Fair Weather Ahead

Keith Lawrence

Copyright © 2012 by Keith Lawrence

Fair Weather Ahead
by Keith Lawrence

Printed in the United States of America

ISBN 9781625092007

All rights reserved solely by the author. The author guarantees all contents are original and do not infringe upon the legal rights of any other person or work. No part of this book may be reproduced in any form without the permission of the author. The views expressed in this book are not necessarily those of the publisher.

Unless otherwise indicated, Bible quotations are taken from The American Standard Version of the Bible.

www.xulonpress.com

Tom & Pat
Thank you for all you do & being a great friend. God Bless

Loves
Keith
Gal 2:20

Contents

Introduction xi

Preface xiii

1. Life-changing Words 25

2. Facing the Giant 30

3. First Breath of Fresh Air 41

4. Thanks for Donors 49

5. Mountain Tops and Valley Lows 54

6. God of Second Chances 61

7. Intestinal Fortitude Defined 67

8. Giving Thanks, Renewing Commitments,
   and Goals Reached 78

9. Thoughts and Comments 92

10. Here We Go Again! 102

11. We Knew This Day Would Come! 129

12. Moving On 143

This book is dedicated to Linda, my loving wife that left us all behind way to soon. Without her bravery and determination this journey would have never been recorded to encourage others.

Special thanks to Betty Black for encouraging me to write this story and for the many hours editing and making suggestions that helped make the goal of completion achievable.

Introduction

The following is my best attempt to present, for anyone interested, the events of an incredible journey that I had the privilege of taking with the most extraordinary person. Everyone might have an idea of how they will react in a crisis, and most of us want to avoid any conflicts, hardships, or just about anything that makes our everyday life more difficult in any way. This is a story about a terrible illness that changed our daily lives and caused many hardships but resulted in a deeper love between two people that had already spent the majority of their lives together. I hope to accurately present the events and provide hope for anyone thinking they have been presented with an unbearable burden or face an unattainable goal. This story is by no means the worst story ever told, and in my opinion our suffering pales in comparison to others. Nevertheless, this story is a testament to the courage, internal fortitude, and the "never give up" attitude of one person. This story, more importantly, is a validation of the power of prayer and how it provides strength, comfort, hope, and life.

Special Thanks to Our Lord and Savior
Jesus Christ

Preface

*D*ecember 1, 1951, was a Saturday that forever changed the lives of a young couple in Austin, Texas. Hank and Charla Sasser were living in a small travel trailer (about twenty feet long) while Hank attended The University of Texas studying to be a petroleum engineer. Linda Kay Sasser was born at St. David's Hospital in Austin. Who could have known how this little bundle of joy would affect so many lives? She would set an example for us all when it came to never giving up against enormous odds in facing an incurable disease.

Hank graduated and was hired by Standard Oil Company (Chevron Oil Company today), and they moved to Monahan, Texas where he was a roustabout for his first assignment. They then transferred to Sherman for two years before moving to Corpus Christi, Texas. Later in his career, they were transferred to an oil camp named Alta Mesa in the middle of nowhere. It was thirty miles south of Falfurrias, forty miles north of Edinburg, and fifteen miles west of Rachael in Texas. Check that out on any map, and you will see it's in the middle of nowhere. Their family had grown to include Linda's sister, Sharon, and a little brother, Charles. Life was not easy living in an oil camp in the middle of huge South Texas ranches. Their friends were limited to the other families that lived in the camp, which would fluctuate with the transfer in and out of employees. There were some core families that stayed long term like the Sasser's, and both parents and kids became good friends.

Daddy's little Girl   **Linda Kay**

To allow for the many stops along the way, the school bus ride to Falfurrias started early in the morning, before sunrise. The bus ride took an hour and fifteen minutes on a good day. Later, when Linda joined the band and stayed after school for practice, the return trip to the house was in the dark of night. School days were not always easy.

The kids liked the country life, and there were many Indians slain as the group would divide up and play cowboys and Indians on most Saturdays and Sundays. It seemed Charles, being the youngest, was always given the role of the Indian and the rest of them would scalp him. Since the girls always dressed him up like a doll in pretty little dresses and shoes, Charles never stood a chance. I even heard about

Preface

a ribbon worn in his hair most of the time until he was old enough to fight back.

Hank was a very frugal man, and while he did make good money as a petroleum engineer, no one could tell. He liked to hunt, and consequently, the main course for the family meal was venison. They ate so much venison that later in life, when the occasion presented itself, Linda wouldn't even touch it. She was burned out on deer meat.

Hank was transferred back to Corpus Christi in late summer of 1968, and other than seeing Linda and Sharon riding around in the little red Jeep, we didn't know each other. I did admire her from afar. Linda and her family had joined Tuloso Midway Baptist Church where we happened to be members, although at the time they joined, I wasn't a real regular attendee. There was a revival in the summer of 1969, and Linda was in charge of filling a pew. She asked me to come and sit in her pew, and I became a regular attender again. Although, I did get to spend that week at the revival around her, we still didn't get to know each other well. I still admired her from a distance.

School had been going for about two weeks, and I guess Linda was transferred to a different class. She walked into my senior government class one day and caught my eye. I'm not sure I had ever seen anyone as beautiful as she was that day; it was if I had seen her for the first time. My partner in crime who sat next to me in the last row made a five-dollar bet with me. He bet me he would take her on a date before I would. So the challenge was on.

Neither one of us had the courage to talk to her because we both felt she was out of our league. Finally, one day he made the comment in front of her that I would have to pay off the five dollars. I asked him why, and he said that Linda had agreed to go with him to the football game. I said, "Oh really? She said she was going with me!" (first liar doesn't stand a chance). So there the three of us stood, and of course neither of us had even talked to her. She looked at him and then at me and said, "Yes, I did tell Keith I would go with him." As they say, the rest is history!

I made the joke for the rest of our lives together that if I could ever find that guy I would give him his five dollars. Linda went on to graduate early and started Del Mar College at midterm of our senior year. We dated off and on but neither one of us was ready to commit to each other yet. We did start dating more regularly after I graduated, and we were together for the summer and winter of 1970. Of course, as with all kids in love, we had a falling out. We had decided to break up and "date other people," as the saying goes. Linda flew out to Denver to spend some time with her cousin. It drove me crazy. I called her and pretty much begged her to come home. She flew back, and I picked her up at the airport and proposed to her. We were married May 7th, 1971 after what most everyone thought was a very short engagement. I thought it was a very long one.

May 7, 1971

Preface

Linda came home from work at Southwestern Bell Telephone one day and announced that we needed to start our family. We had been married four years, and I was having lots of fun, and the idea didn't set to well with me, but then I didn't get a vote. Colby came along July 29, 1975, when I was on a job in Refugio, Texas working as an electrician. I borrowed my boss's truck and used the opportunity to drive a hundred miles an hour and still almost didn't get there in time for his arrival.

We took a job in Marion, Kansas and moved there in January of 1976. That following winter was the worst Kansas had seen in fifty years. There were snow drifts higher than the vehicles, and I didn't adapt very well. There was one stretch of cold weather that lasted for thirty-five days, and the temperature did not get above 32 degrees. Linda and Colby did not leave the house for the entire thirty-five days. We rented an old frame house with ten-foot ceilings and leaky windows. Supposedly, the three houses that sat next to each other once belonged to Abraham Lincoln. I don't know if that was true or not, but it made an interesting story; they were very old houses. It had an old floor furnace that Linda and Colby would place a chair on top of and wrap up in a blanket. She would read books to him all day long. One time Colby left one of his riding toys on the heater and it melted the plastic wheels. From then on it was known as the heater monster.

I approached my boss and told him that these snow shoes didn't fit these south Texas feet and as soon as it thawed out, I was heading south. He laughed since he was from Texas also and said they would move us back to Corpus Christi and give me my old job back. We had the moving people lined up to come Monday morning and load everything. We hadn't told anyone in Corpus that we were coming back because we wanted it to be a surprise. Unfortunately, we had our own surprise coming.

The phone rang Saturday night, and it was one of Linda's uncles. He told me that Linda's dad had been killed in a hunting accident. It turns out while they were setting up a deer blind, the rope broke, and the blind started falling. As Hank rushed to get everyone else out of the way, he tripped and fell, and the blind fell on him. The weight of the blind hit right on his chest and broke an artery in his heart. He was dead before they arrived at the Alice hospital.

We loaded up and headed to Texas with everything still sitting in the house. Our landlord oversaw the packing and loading of all our possessions that arrived in Corpus Christi ten days later. We did not have a house at the time and were bouncing back and forth between my parent's house and Linda's mom's house. We would stay about two weeks and then move to the other one when our welcome wore out.

Kenda arrived July 24, 1978, and Linda said, "We are through having kids; you need to go see the doctor." Once again, I didn't get a vote. The same doctor that delivered our kids and me now got to perform a vasectomy to end the string of customers in our family.

I could go on and on about the different situations and predicaments I would get us into. I found myself always apologizing to her for another situation I had created, but she would always graciously say, "Oh, living with you is just an adventure!" Linda was a real unusual blend of engineer and romantic. She could work as hard as any man and longer than most people I've ever known. Once she made up her mind to do something, there was no turning back, and she wasn't afraid to tackle anything. It was amazing to watch her figure out a problem and apply the solution. Since she was an accomplished seamstress, it was a real treasure to get any of her handiwork, especially the corduroy shirts. Also, she crocheted and designed her own patterns. She created

Preface

cryptic instructions that produced beautiful baby blankets. She would spend more than forty hours working on those treasures to give to family members and friends to bring their babies home from the hospital.

I don't know what else to say except she was an extraordinary person who everyone could not help but like and admire.

Pa Sasser, Colby and Linda

Linda and Kenda

Linda, Colby and Keith

Linda & her mom, Charla

Preface

Linda & grandma Hannsen

Linda & Charla

Linda & sister Sharon

Girls day out, Joan, Linda, Kenda, Charlotte, Carol

Preface

Linda our 25th wedding anniversary

Chapter One

Life-changing Words

*L*ife was mostly normal. Linda and I had settled into an empty nest and for the most part were handling the realization that it would be a nonglamorous push through middle age into the "golden" years and simply growing old together. Most of our time together had been blessed with good health. Usually, the family did not visit the doctor outside of yearly checkups, which often turned into five-year checkups. Shots or any other medical procedures only surpassed our dislike for pills as simple as aspirin. Like most people we didn't like introducing chemicals or pain into our bodies.

I guess you have to go back to the summer of 1999 to understand how all of this started. I had always desired to live on lakefront property. Linda had grown up in the country and didn't want to give up the convenience of city living. We lived in the suburbs, but we were one block from the grocery store, four miles from work, and she loved the house where we lived. My personal dislike of city living had been growing with the increase in taxes, insurance, and the closing in of people all around me. Having grown up in the area where we lived, it was difficult to see that it had grown to include strip malls, corner convenience stores, and houses.

Fair Weather Ahead

These were the vacant fields where I use to hunt rabbits, ride horses, and generally stomp around as a kid. Maybe it was my middle-age crazy period, but finally one Saturday as I read another letter from the city, I blurted out "That's it. Get in the car. We're moving."

West, out of town, across the river bridge was where I longed to be. We drove around all the surrounding areas most of Saturday afternoon. We visited all the small towns and farming communities, including some dead-end roads in the middle of plowed fields. Neither one of us saw anything that began to spark our interest. We headed back to town, and as we crossed the river bridge, I said with a tone of disgust, "I guess we're stuck where we are." Linda's next comment almost caused a wreck. "Why don't we look at the lake?" I couldn't believe what I had just heard. "I thought you wouldn't live on the lake," I said. She replied, "As long as it's not the last place we live." Well, I found the first turnaround and back over the river bridge we went.

The story of the "river lots" is another book in and of itself. We did buy a trailer and moved onto the lot as we worked converting a fishing cabin to a full-time habitable mansion of "my" dreams. Linda had been struggling with allergies, and the move to the river only made them worse. She had been seeing an ear, nose, and throat (ENT) doctor for almost a year, and the injections she had been giving herself didn't seem to be helping. The usual symptoms—runny nose, itchy eyes, and generally run-down feeling—were also accompanied by a persistent dry cough. I know how aggravating the constant coughing was to me, and can't imagine how it must have driven Linda crazy. The ENT doctor had seen some fibrosis in her lungs but basically disregarded it and commented to Linda's question about it that, "Oh it's just some scarring that we don't know where it came from." This was early 1999.

Life-Changing Words

By January 2001, the coughing continued, and I told Linda to go find another doctor to see if anything could be done to rid her of the cough. This was Linda's first relief from some of the allergy symptoms, as she started a series of shots with an allergist. After testing and finding out Linda was allergic to a list of items just the opposite of what most people have reactions to, a full-strength dose of carpet grass, oak, and a laundry list of everyday invaders were introduced to her body. Thirty days of daily trips and six months of weekly visits for shots had tremendously improved her condition with the allergy symptoms, but the cough continued.

Directed by her allergist, Linda made an appointment with a local pulmonary specialist, Dr.Geneser. Her first visit included an X-ray that would finally and officially identify the cause of the persistent cough. Dr. Geneser made another appointment for Linda and told her to bring her husband. I can remember thinking, *Why does he want me there? This can't involve me. I don't have time for this.* Boy was I wrong!

Dr. Geneser is a very serious, direct, and to-the-point doctor. In the years we have known him, I have made him laugh only twice, well under my average, and that makes for a tough crowd. He looked me straight in the eyes and said something that would change our lives forever. He told us Linda had idiopathic pulmonary fibrous (IPF), three words I wish I had never heard. It took a while for the next sentence to sink in when he said, "It's an incurable lung disease." I really don't remember what I said, but I remember thinking, *This is a mistake. They have Linda's x-rays mixed up with someone else's or they misread the x-ray. After all, we're just talking about a little cough here, it can't be that bad.* But when he showed us the x-rays, it was. He was able to find some healthy lung in the x-ray and showed us the difference in the part that was involved by the disease and the part that was not.

It's ironic that I don't recall most of our conversation on the way home or even for the next week or so. It was like this was going to go away, and everything would be all right. I guess we both must have been in some form of denial. Here was someone that had been in perfect health all of her life, and then one day the doctor says, "incurable disease." Pulmonary fibrous, simply stated, is the body attacking itself. The disease causes inflammation in the lungs and the body, in an attempt to rid itself of the problem and causes scarring to occur. The scarring is on the outside of the lung and impedes the transfer of oxygen to the blood and gases out of the blood. The exchange area is blocked. The disease in not cancer, but it is like cancer in that once it starts eating away at the lung, it doesn't stop until it's totally involved.

Idiopathic simply means the origin is unknown. Eighty-five percent of the people that contract pulmonary fibrous never know where they got it. I struggled with that for a long time. Several subsequent visits consisted of me drilling Dr. Geneser about where this came from and how this happened. I wanted to go get whatever caused this and beat it up. Dr. Geneser finally grew tired of my insistent badgering and said, "Look, you are going to have to accept that you will never know how she got this and get on with dealing with it." He added most of the people that get cancer never know how they got it. I put it aside.

Dr. Geneser's description of himself is a small town pulmonologist digging around in the dirt. He said a condition this big needed more resources than he had access to. He ordered a biopsy of the lung, which positively identified the disease. Since the procedure-apparently cut through a nerve, this was a terrible experience that proved to be ten times more painful than an actual lung transplant. Linda came

Life-Changing Words

out of the recovery room in excruciating pain that lasted for weeks.

I'll never forget when they finally brought her out of the recovery room; she was hurting and plenty mad. They had left her on the operating gurney too long, and when they moved her over to the bed to bring her to the room they hurt her badly during the transfer. She was in a lot of pain, and when they arrived at the room, she told the nurses not to touch her, that her husband would move her to the bed. Of course, I moved her over to the bed. It wasn't a good experience at all! This was our first dealing with the local hospital, but I will say they did improve. Before it was all said and done, we were very happy overall with the nurses and the hospital.

Chapter Two
Facing the Giant

Dr. Geneser referred us to Dr. Frost at Methodist Hospital in Houston. Dr. Frost is a Canadian who is world-renowned for her work with transplants and dealing with pulmonary diseases. We started traveling to Houston once a month and were considered for some blind testing but missed the deadline. Dr. Frost is involved in a lot of testing and the use of experimental drugs that combat lung diseases. Interferon is a cancer drug that, when added with Prednisone, can be effective against pulmonary fibrous. So far, the testing had been done in England, and the FDA had not approved the mixture for use in the United States as an option for pulmonary fibrous. Shortly after we missed the first blind test, however, the FDA approved the testing in the United States, and Linda was in the first group that was tested.

Update e-mails began to flow August 29, 2002, to the first sixteen people on the list. In order to inform them of Linda's condition, the list grew over time and eventually increased to just under fifty people who I sent updates to and God only knows how many people the updates were forwarded to. In the first e-mail, I informed people that we had another good month. The pulmonary function test (PFT) stayed the same for another month. Dr. Frost had more good news. The blind study testing for Interferon, Gamma was back, and it looked like it would be an effective treatment for UIP. Usual interstitial pneumonia (UIP) is a form of lung disease characterized by progressive scarring of both lungs. The scarring (fibrosis) involves the supporting framework (interstitium) of the lung. UIP is classified as a form of interstitial lung disease. The term "usual" refers to the fact that UIP is the most common form of interstitial fibrosis. "Pneumonia" indicates "lung abnormality," which includes fibrosis and inflammation.

When administered with 10 mg. of Prednisone (steroids), there had been significant arresting of the progression of the UIP. This would not repair any damage, but it might lift recently laid down inflammations. Linda was now down to 10 mg. of Prednisone, which was actually what we wanted to mix with the Interferon. The easiest way to think about it was, this was the best chance we had to not only stop the spreading of scarring, but it could remove recently attached inflammation. Dr. Frost was very excited about the results that just came out that week. Since they would not pay for experimental drugs, and I didn't think the FDA had approved this drug for this treatment, we submitted results to the insurance company. This was a very expensive process. Flint Hills Resources (FHR) employees can be grateful for such good insurance, because once it was approved, they would cover the cost of the drug. The plan was for Linda to start taking three injections a week and gradually work up to the full dosage. We would continue our monthly trips for about three more months till the desired dosage was obtained. After that we had hope to reduce our Houston visits to once every three months. We would continue regular visits to our local specialist.

At this point, things looked better than any time since we had found out about Linda's condition. Dr. Frost continued to call Linda's case an atypical one. Linda's lungs were bigger than most people her size, and she continued to have good oxygen transfer. I wondered if she already had big lungs or got them after all the prayers. We continued to appreciate everyone's support and prayers. The battle would continue on, but I felt like we were in better shape than ever before, and all the support had helped in that happening.

Here is a little bit about Interferon, Gamma (Systemic).

Gamma Interferon (GAM-a inter-FEER-on) is a synthetic (man-made) version of a substance naturally produced by cells in the body to help fight infections and tumors. It is commonly used to treat chronic granulomatous disease and osteoporosis. The side effects are minimal and usually occur concurrently with the injections. They can cause a flu-like reaction, with aching muscles, fever and chills, and headache. It is suggested to take acetaminophen before each dose of Interferon to help prevent problems with body temperature going too high. While these side effects may seem bad, they are nothing compared to where we could have gone with the large doses of Prednisone.

There is no way I could possibly include all the email responses, but I felt like a few would give a good idea of what kind of support we received from them. Here are a few.

"Great news! God sure is awesome, ain't he???!!! I'll continue to pray for Linda and you. Keep the faith."

"Thank you very much for the update, sounds like everyone's prayers and thoughts are helping, we'll continue."

"Thanks for the update. It is exciting to hear about answered prayers. We will keep you and Linda on our list. Hope that I'm not taking this out of context, but I committed it to memory last week." James 5:16 *Confess therefore your sins one to another, and pray one for another, that ye may be healed. The supplication of a righteous man availeth much in its working.*

The only ways to determine if the disease is stable, progressing, or regressing are x-rays and pulmonary function tests or PFT. We drove to Houston once a month for x-rays and PFTs, and after ninety days it was apparent the drug cocktail would not be effective in Linda's case. Meanwhile, we had the good fortune of what some might call a chance encounter, but I don't believe in coincidences. Linda's sister Sharon is a nurse in Austin. She had worked with a friend who she ran into at lunch one day. They sat down and began sharing what was currently going on in their lives. It seems her friend had worked as an organ donor solicitor. I don't know much about this type of work other than they educate people about the need for organ donors and try to sign people up to donate. Well, Sharon's reply was, "I have a sister who might need a transplant, and she is going to a doctor in Houston." His immediate reply was, "She needs to go to San Antonio. Dr. Louis Angel is the doctor there, and he and the program are great."

We made the appointment to meet Dr. Angel, and after a visit in Houston drove straight to San Antonio. His comment was lung transplants were not a selective surgery and they carefully considered each case and performed transplants on patients for whom a transplant would improve quality of life. He started Linda's file and said come back when we were closer to needing a transplant.

The signature pattern of pulmonary fibrous is the three usual lengths of progression. Once the disease is first contracted, five, ten, or fifteen years are the common duration for life expectancy. Not knowing for sure when Linda contracted the disease, we could only try to think back when the coughing started. With the x-ray of the ENT confirming the disease in 2000, we could only guess that by now she was in her third year of infection. Dr. Frost had told us that the disease could go along for a period of time and hardly change at all and then one day take a dive like a rock in a well. The progression is different with each case and person. The decline in PFTs had been steady but rather slow. We made our regular visit to Dr. Frost and there hadn't been much of a change. It would take three to six months before we could tell if the Interferon would be effective or not. Some tests were the same from month to month, and we thought some were even better than the last. The PFT results were off a little bit, but we all felt like it was due to sore ribs Linda had from coughing attacks. Since she had been off of the large doses of steroids she had been more susceptible to uncontrollable coughing attacks. The result was sore ribs and lots of pain associated with breathing, especially during the PFT when she was required to inhale and exhale large amounts of air. Then, towards the end of 2002, the decline was obvious. Dr. Frost started talking seriously about getting Linda on the transplant list right away because the waiting period in Houston was thirteen to fifteen months. Since we might need to exercise the transplant options in San Antonio, the doctor ordered us to go ahead and get the pre-qualifying work and physical completed with Dr. Angel. We then officially transferred Linda's care to Dr. Angel. We had a visit with the local specialist, an appointment with Dr. Angel on October 31st, and then went back to Dr. Frost the third week of December. There was not a whole lot to share at that time. Since the prednisone had been reduced to just ten mg. per day, things were a lot better mentally. The three injections per week started out badly. Since Linda was taking Tylenol and drinking lots of water with the injections, the side effects were greatly reduced and tolerable. Through many e-mails and phone calls, I continued to thank everyone for the wonderful support and prayers we were receiving.

We continued regular visits to Houston and to the local pulmonary specialist. The side effects of the prednisone were weight gain and a puffy face. I don't need to tell anyone how those two symptoms could affect anyone, especially all the women who have been molded to believe their beauty is in their outward appearance. The side effects of the interferon were flu-like symptoms that reduced appetite and just made the shot days, which were three times a week, like a two-day battle with the flu. Needless to say spirits were low, and the questions in our minds were never ending. Depression for both of us became a continuous battle, as well. I tried my best to never let Linda see my own doubts and fears and never let on to her that I doubted that anything we tried would be effective.

The continued support of my co-workers, friends, and family was instrumental in the support I passed on to Linda. I felt like support from a person's immediate as well as extended family and the church family is essential. This is where we are supposed to turn for encouragement and the feeling that you're not in this alone. We were blessed and to this day still receive the support of a work family that exceeds anything I have ever heard of. My support from co-workers, management, and just about everyone in the Flint Hills Resources organization has been above and beyond the call. I can't imagine anyone going through something like this without support from his or her employer.

Long days of fighting fatigue, the urge to throw up (sometimes more than an urge), and the never-ending questions in Linda's mind, as well as mine, made the end of each day worse. It seemed both of us were more susceptible to the onslaught of doubts and fears at bedtime. Many nights were spent crying and asking questions that we knew had no answers for us. Linda's two biggest desires were to live long enough to see her grandchildren and also see Colby graduate from college. Fear of death wasn't as big an issue as the fear of not being able to share life together. We were able to wrestle through those emotions most nights, and Linda's strength probably helped me get through those experiences more than my strength helped her. Many nights were spent sleeping on damp pillows, and while I never got angry with God, I sure wondered a time or two if he knew what he was doing. — or allowing to happen

The time from November 2002 to about February 2003 seemed to just drag on and on. I know the times between visits were long periods of ups and downs, and I often look back and regret we didn't do things differently. I wish we would have been more adventuresome and maybe made more memories together instead of fighting my dream at the river that turned into a nightmare. I'm not sure Linda would have felt like it or if she had the strength, but I should have recognized the finality of the situation and tried to be more sensitive to her needs earlier.

People continued to ask for updates on our situation. I let folks know about our activities from the last couple of weeks. Our visit to Houston did not have good numbers. The PFT test indicated that the diffusion of oxygen to the blood stream was not happening as it should. There had been a steady decline from the first test last year. This was a good indication, along with other results, that the interferon was not being effective. Dr. Frost took Linda off of the interferon immediately. There was a new experimental drug called Tracleer that was being administered. Dr. Frost checked to see if Linda met the protocol, because if she did, Linda would be in the test. Dr. Frost said at this point we didn't have much to lose.

We visited Dr. Angel in San Antonio, and he had Linda walk the halls with an oximeter attached to her finger. This also proved that she was not getting the oxygen she needed into her blood stream. Her saturation level dipped into the low 80s and should never have gone below 90. Dr. Angel said she must be tough and not complain much. Linda told him she was a Texas Girl, and they were all tough. Dr. Angel said she was not a normal patient and was atypical. Sounds familiar because that's the same thing Dr. Frost said. What's interesting about it is, I had the chance to compare notes with others in the hospitals and Linda was responding differently than patients they had. I met a man who had a transplant five weeks earlier, and he was looking pretty good. We compared some test numbers with Linda's and one of the numbers on her report was a 30 (for this story it doesn't matter what it represents) and he told me when he reached as low as a 40 he was begging for oxygen. Linda had not felt like she needed any oxygen yet. Dr. Angel prescribed oxygen and said Linda probably needed to be sleeping with it on. We had our own oximeter ordered and started watching the oxygen levels daily. We had another appointment in San Antonio Friday the 28th. It was the preliminary work for a transplant. They would perform all the tests except for the heart catheter. The heart catheter would take place at the time of a transplant, if it became necessary. Outside of a total miracle, which had not been ruled out, or the new drug working, which might be the miracle, a transplant was pretty imminent. No one knows when, but San Antonio had been doing well moving folks up on their waiting list. They had a guy last month that received a lung within twenty three hours of his need. Their average time was about one month.

    The details of the first four months of 2003 seem to have left me. I remember long drives to Houston and what seemed like many hours sitting around hospitals waiting on something or someone. Lunches together and discussions in the privacy of our vehicle were highlights of the day. By then Linda's desire to sleep ninety percent of the travel time and the desire to eat were overriding any enjoyment she

Fair Weather Ahead

could get from time spent together. I know now events in our life outside of the health issues don't even get a spot in my memory. I know we must have celebrated Thanksgiving, Christmas, Linda's birthday, and mine during this time span, but I couldn't tell you where or how we celebrated.

We were getting much closer to the transplant procedure. The heart catheter went well, with no complications. The lung pressure was good, and the heart chambers were good. This was the last test before we could get on the transplant list. We were supposed to go to Houston for a 9:00 AM Tuesday, April 22, 2003 appointment and then received a call to go back to San Antonio Wednesday morning at 9:00 AM. We hoped that would be the day they would put us on the transplant list. Linda was on oxygen full time now.

Things started moving fast during this week. We traveled to Houston Monday night for an appointment the next day. We met with Dr. Frost in Houston after more PFT tests earlier that morning. I really liked the way she handled herself, and you never had to wonder what she was thinking. She said Linda's numbers were falling like a rock, and it (the disease) was moving like a freight train. She said it was time to get the transplant because that was our only option. There was another blind study starting with another experimental drug, but Linda's numbers were already too bad to get into the program. It surprised me and almost came as a shock hearing her say the words, "It's time!" We had talked about this day and had known it would come, but it still came as a shock to hear the doctor say it. During the visit, Dr. Frost had another doctor follow her around as a learning experience. They had left the room to look at X-rays, and when they returned Linda was on the phone with San Antonio. I asked Dr. Frost how could it be that Linda could be a week away from a transplant and still look so good. She said the doctor with her asked the same thing when they stepped outside the room. We had been told that we could draw a straight line

Facing The Giant

for an indefinite amount of time and then for no reason over night the disease would just take over. That had happened. The numbers had been declining for the last nine months, but the past month had been more dramatic, and time was an issue.

The tour of Texas was done. I don't know how those truck drivers do it! We met Dr. Angel in San Antonio Wednesday morning, and after a walking test, where the oxygen observation rate is monitored, it was apparent to Dr. Angel it was time. There were many numbers and different factors that figured in, but one of the most obvious was the lung volume percentage of expected capacity was down to fifty percent. Nine months ago it was eighty percent, but more important than that was the ability to transfer oxygen to the blood stream which had dropped off the table. Those were all the bad numbers. The good numbers were ahead. We were the second person on the list, and although Linda's blood type was a little rare, (B) they could use an (O) blood type organ. The average lead time for an organ to become available was fifty-four days. Sometimes it could happen in a week. We had a few final details to work out with the insurance company, but that wouldn't be a problem. The survival rate for the first year was ninety-four percent, and the last thirty two transplants had been successful. So those numbers were in our favor. There were really three stages to this. First, you had to live through the surgery, then, get through the recovery, and then make it through the rehab. It's different for everyone. One guy received a transplant and left the hospital in four days. One guy was in the hospital for three months, but he has had the transplant for twelve years, so you just don't know what to expect. We were to go to San Antonio May 2 for a class to meet other transplant recipients and to learn what to expect before and after. I knew our lifestyles would change for a while, but we were confident we would get back to normal some time down the road. Just didn't know how long the road would be!

Once again, I thanked everyone for all the prayers and support. They had helped us get this far, and I knew we would need all them to help us get through the rest of this ordeal. The call could come at any time from a week to months from now. Since the progression had picked up, we were hoping and praying it would be sooner. We were ready to get started so we could get finished and put this chapter behind us. I promised to keep everyone up to date as things changed.

Chapter Three

First Breath of Fresh Air

On Sunday, April 27, 2005, I found myself at the church and up front at the altar call. I don't even remember going up or the last half of the sermon. I knew I needed to find some strength I didn't currently have. My pastor, Brother Mark Miller, prayed with me, and there was an immediate peace about the entire procedure. It was as if the building had been lifted off of my shoulders. I can't tell you today what Mark's prayer sounded like except that I remember he asked for peace and strength. I had been wandering in the wilderness, and here was another time I came running back to a merciful God. It was a great time, and I don't understand how anyone gets through these ordeals without God. Here is an actual e-mail someone sent me that I saved. I don't save many of the little phrases or stories, but this one really touched me, and I kept it. Notice the date I received it.

03/01/02
God didn't promise days without pain, laughter without sorrow, sun without rain,

But He did promise strength for the day, comfort for the tears, and light for the way.

We received the call Monday morning about 10:00 AM that all the details were completed, and we were officially on the list. The call could come at any time from now until maybe months from now. I realized that if the disease continued at the same rate of decline that Linda probably wouldn't make it to July. That was my nonprofessional opinion, and no one could say for sure, but she was getting worse pretty quickly. I'll never forget how she kept denying she needed oxygen, but the day she decided she needed it, she wanted it right then. For me personally, that was a big turning point. It seemed it was the final sign that the disease was winning. I knew all along that day would come, but it overwhelmed me so that walks around the neighborhood became regular events so I could hide my uncontrollable crying.

We never made the classes that were going to tell us what to expect and where to find support from other transplant families. We did, however, meet lots of very thoughtful transplant patients who offered much encouragement. One in particular led me to a website called "Second Wind." I found a book there that tells the story of many successful transplants. This book was a tremendous help to Linda and me as we read about all the successful transplants. This person really connected with Linda, and he was a huge encourager who had had many struggles that included never-ending migraine headaches. He has since passed on, and he is missed.

I tried to get out an e-mail several times from a borrowed laptop. I was staying in an old rest home that had been converted into a place for transplant patient families to stay. They only charged thirty dollars a night to stay, and it was always full. It had its good points in that there were other families staying there that understood what you were going through. The bad points were other families were there that were going through the same things, and all of them didn't turn out so well. It was a time to support each other, but I didn't go back after my first week's stay. It was more depressing than the benefit of being there. There were just too many sad stories, and the majority of the stories didn't include any type of faith.

It was difficult to see moms, dads, brothers, sisters, other family members, and friends dealing with the anxiety that lives in the lives of transplant families. The most difficult for me to watch were the spouses, especially the women. They had relied on their husbands for so many years, and now the idea of losing them was very painful. Watching all the emotions from one end of the spectrum to the other and those that had no God in their lives can't be explained. They were mad at God, if they believed there was one, but a lot of them didn't think a loving God would allow this to happen. The occasional believer who came along was refreshing, and we encouraged each other since most of the others were not interested in speaking of God things.

It was about 11:30 by the time I arrived at the room, and I really wanted to get an e-mail out to everyone, but I had so much trouble as you will see in the following account.

Lawrence's Believe It or Not. OK: there must have been something or someone not wanting this information published. It was the third attempt to send the e-mail. I had about twenty-five minutes typed on the laptop Friday night when the battery died, and I lost all that work. I just tried again and had ninety minutes typed when I bumped the wrong button and lost it. I tried Word the next time and saved about every three minutes so I could get this one out to everyone that night.

Do What? Are you kidding!! Praise God!! Amazing!! If I had a dollar for each time I heard those phrases or comments that week I would be a millionaire. It was a remarkable ride and to not believe that it was all orchestrated by someone

Fair Weather Ahead

would be a mistake. I believe God had it all laid out, and we just had to ask for it. I'll share the events of that week, and you decide for yourself. There were other events leading up to the week that also confirmed divine intervention but due to donor sensitivity I am not at liberty to share those events with you at this time. Maybe someday I can and I will, but just trust me when I say this donor was "selected" for Linda. The events leading up to the new lung and Linda getting together on Wednesday, April 30, 2003, was no coincidence.

Monday, April 28, 2003, at 10:00 AM we received the call from our caseworker that the insurance had agreed to everything, and we were officially on the list. We just settled in for the wait, knowing that the average wait for San Antonio was fifty-four days. I had already wondered how some people wait one, two, or even three years on some lists.

Tuesday, April 29, 2003, at 11:30 PM, we received the call from the transplant team to come to San Antonio between 7:00 and 7:30 AM. The hospital might have a match but would not know until morning. There are lots of dry runs due to mismatches and nonuseable organs. I started to pack and asked Linda, "What do you need?" She said, "What else will I need; they will give me a gown!" I called my brother and sister. There would be no more sleeping that night, and since I had watched the basketball playoffs until 10:45 PM, it was a short night.

Wednesday, April 30, 2003, at 2:10 AM, we left the house for San Antonio. We arrived at the hospital parking lot at 4:15 AM. Since they were only thirty minutes behind us, we waited for my brother and sister-in-law. We tried to nap while we waited, but forget that. We walked on to the twelfth floor (transplant floor) at 5:00 AM. They started working on Linda right away. They drew fifteen vials of blood before she could sit down. After checking, prodding, poking, and sticking her for about an hour, they left her alone. Then we waited. We should have known something by 7:30, 8:30, or

10:00 AM. Then the word came it was a match, and the deal was on, but instead of one lung there were two. Our specialist wanted two but the surgeon wanted to transplant one. After much debate and discussion the decision was made to transplant only one. The right lung had excessive bruising and no one wanted to take a chance. They should operate at 1:00 PM. The nine family members present circled the bed and prayed over Linda. They finally came and got her at 2:00 PM. The operating room nurse called us at 2:30 PM and said they had made the first incision. She called back at 4:00 PM and said the old lung was out, and they were sewing in the new one. Dr. Johnson, one of nine surgeons, came out about 5:30 PM and said all went well and the new lung was "pristine." We liked that description. The nurse called back and said if we wanted to see Linda, we would need to go upstairs to ICU. It was 6:00 PM, three-and-one-half hours from beginning to end—unbelievable! When we walked into ICU, she had tubes and machines hooked up everywhere. Colby and I were talking, and I said at least she couldn't hear us. Wrong. She started shaking her head back and forth. I said, "Linda can you feel Colby touching your hand?" She shook her head yes. I said, "Is everything all right?" She shook her head no. The problem was trying to figure out what was wrong. Hands tied and a breathing tube down her throat, there was no way to communicate. The nurses gave her a pencil and paper later, and we finally realized the tube in her mouth was pinching her lip between her teeth. The pain had been so bad it brought her out of the anesthesia. The nurses told her that it had to be tight to keep her from coughing it up and tearing out her vocal cords. They knocked her out again for the night. Dr. Angel told me she was doing great, and if it had not been so late and all the doctors weren't leaving, he would have removed the ventilator that night, but he opted to wait for morning. Dr. New, another surgeon, informed us that the new lung started working almost immediately, and the blood gases were good from the get-go. Dr. New agreed that if that continued, she would come off the ventilator the next day. She really wanted the tube out of her throat.

Since we were not in a big hurry on Thursday, May 1, 2003, we arrived a little late at 9:15 AM. We figured Linda would still be out and never thought otherwise. WRONG AGAIN! We walked into the room, and she was sitting up in bed. "Where have you been?" she asked. I knew she was all right then. Dr. Johnson came by and asked," Are you the woman that had a transplant yesterday?" Linda said, "That's what y'all tell me!" At 1:00 PM, she was released from ICU, but no rooms were available. Two chest tubes and a couple of drip lines were all that remained. Since the tube was not pinching her lip, Linda had no pain. She continually denied the request to give her morphine—no pain. She was finally moved her to a room at 10:00 PM. It had been a long day. I had been up for almost twenty-three hours, but surprisingly I was only tired, not sleepy. Everything was going great, and there were a lot more details I wanted to relate, but not that night. This was only step one of a long three-step process. Linda's new lung was working, and her numbers were good once again. I thanked everyone for their support and especially all the prayers. People asked about sending flowers, but I let them know that flowers were not allowed on the twelfth floor. Cards were welcome, and I let them know where to send them. All in all, things had gone above expectations.

Friday, May 2, 2003, she ate a breakfast that consisted of scrambled eggs and muffins. Doctors came through all day long and were amazed at how she was doing. One doctor commented that how this all came together is a miracle and what a unique situation this was. I told one doctor "This is what happens when a million people are praying for one woman." At 10:00 AM one chest tube was removed with hardly any drainage. At 4:00 PM, Linda was walking the halls.

First Breath Of Fresh Air

Saturday, May 3, 2003, at 10:00 AM, the last chest tube was removed. I assisted on this one; it wasn't that bad. Dr. Angel said if we wanted, we could go home after a couple of hours of observation. We were cleared to leave at 1:00 PM. With the paper work all completed, we rolled out the front door at 5:00 PM. We made it home, and the first night back was uneventful. Linda and I slept all night.

Sunday, May 4, 2003, we spent about an hour working on pills. Really, it was not as bad as I thought it would be. There were about thirteen morning pills, two at midday, eight in the evening, and two at bedtime. The new prayer request was NO rejection/NO infection. We had to be very careful of doses of medication and the time for all of them. There was a number that had to be maintained in the blood that represented the anti-rejection drug strength. We were scheduled to go to San Antonio every Tuesday for the next three months to have checkups. They would also run PFTs and other tests. We had an extra trip on Friday to remove the staples.

Just a warning: we were by no means out of the woods. The anti-rejection drugs could cause some problems. I knew one story where the girl threw up continually for about six weeks. So far so good! There would be about a month of high dose steroids again, and we all knew how Linda hated that last time. Good thing was, they drop off pretty fast after a month and are reduced to just 10mg. a day.

This was a tremendous story, and I couldn't tell everyone how much they had helped in being a part of it with us. We couldn't have made it without support and prayers. I told Linda I wish I could find out just how many churches, Sunday schools, deacon bodies, and individuals had been praying for us. It made the journey almost pleasant. I told someone only Linda could make a lung transplant an enjoyable event. We all know who really supplied the joy.

My sister said she felt like she was living right in the middle of a miracle. Everyone was in the middle of it as well. We offered thanks from the bottom of our hearts, and I knew God was going to bless all for their concern and prayers. I would continue to keep all posted of any changes.

Chapter Four

Thanks for Donors

The first incision was made, and I had several family members present in the waiting room. I never felt that this whole thing would not work. I had great confidence in the doctors, family, and friends who were near and knew God was in control. Little did we know that the donor had been in the same hospital for a week. Even today I'm reluctant to tell the entire story of our donor. I will say he and his family were very gracious and thoughtful of others when they signed their entire family up as donors. This was a very young man, and he made a compassionate statement that would change the lives of people he would never meet and give life to others because of his unselfishness. I doubt very seriously that he considered he would have the chance to be such a big part of so many people's lives so early in his own life. His death was a tremendous tragedy and loss to his family. I will never be able to comprehend the loss of a child, but I do believe his gift was not in vain and provided hope for others. His life, although short on this earth, had a remarkable impact on many. "Thank you" is all I can say for now. I will thank you in person someday.

Linda and I wanted to send out a letter about the donor and information on how to help in this situation. This actual letter was sent out May 13, 2003.

The relationship between a donor family and a recipient family is very different and can be fragile. There are emotions in both families that include mourning for the deceased loved one and great joy for the new life given and received. Please, realize the sensitive nature of this information and share it with discernment. Texas is a big state, but sometimes South Texas can be very small. Often one talks to someone that knows someone and before you know it, there is a connection, and we really want to prevent any type of connection being made. The Texas Organ Sharing Alliance recommends that the two families not communicate and should not even try to find out about the other, particularly this early. With that preface I would like to share some information regarding our donor family. Due to the high profile of the incident around our donor's accident, we found out who the donor is. We are trying to be very careful about that information and are thinking of the donor family, as much as ourselves, by keeping this confidential. We do know that this is a young family and the unexpected funeral cost would be a burden for any of us. To help with the cost of the funeral there is a fund set up at a Credit Union in San Antonio. Linda has made arrangements, which will keep those donations confidential, for anyone wishing to donate to the fund. I know there were many people wanting to send flowers and couldn't and still can't due to Linda's condition. We think it would be a great idea for anyone that wanted to spend money on flowers to send that money to the funeral fund. Of course it would be great to send money to the fund regardless of your flower intentions.

In an effort to make this as anonymous as possible, I have given postage-paid addressed envelopes to an officer in the

Thanks For Donors

credit union organization. She will receive these donations and make the deposit into the funeral fund. There will be no way to connect the donation to the person giving the donation. For those on this mailing list or for anyone that does not have ability to come by my office, I will provide the address at the bottom of this letter. Since these types of accounts are only kept open for ninety days, the deadline to donate to this fund is July 24th. We feel this would be a great help to this family, which was so generous to fifty other families. That's right, by allowing their loved one to be a donor, fifty people have been recipients of this family's generosity.

That reminds me to encourage everyone that reads this letter to make sure your family knows of your intentions to be a donor. We have learned that no matter what kind of card you carry in your pocket stating your desire to be a donor, the surviving family has the say in whether you will be a donor. I have always known of donor programs but never really thought that someday I would need to depend on it as we have. The same could happen to any of you as well. Hopefully, it will never happen to you, but just think of the life you could give someone else with those parts that you think are wore out and no good. It's life changing. Please communicate to your loved ones that you wish to be recycled, it's the cool thing to do.

Security Service Federal Credit Union
PO Box 691510
San Antonio Tx. 78269-9913

Responses to the letter:

While you were praying there, we were praying here. Ain't God good??!!!!
Keith added, "I love living in South Texas"

Probably won't get this immediately, but wanted to let Linda and you know we are praying for you. Just woke up out of a dead sleep and was thinking of you. The real prayer warriors in our household are Iris and Jake (my oldest) and not a day goes by without them mentioning your family.

Proverbs 3:1–6
My son, forget not my law; But let thy heart keep my commandments:
For length of days, and years of life, And peace, will they add to thee.
Let not kindness and truth forsake thee: Bind them about thy neck; Write them upon the tablet of thy heart:
So shalt thou find favor and good understanding In the sight of God and man.
Trust in Jehovah with all thy heart, And lean not upon thine own understanding:
In all thy ways acknowledge him, And he will direct thy paths.

Your brother in Christ,
Dean

That was one of my favorite of all the responses. I like it so much I printed it out, and it is still on my keyboard where I see it all day every day. I tried to keep the responses anonymous, but some of the names might give this one away.

On May 13, 2003, I informed everyone that everything continued to be better than expected. Tuesday was our second weekly check-up. PFTs continued to get better; little or no side effects occurred from the anti-rejection drugs. They reduced both the anti-rejection drugs and the steroids. That made Linda's day. She did need an infusion drug administered because the new guest lung had a virus that she did not have. Don't even ask me for the name, but apparently the majority of us have the virus, but it lies dormant all of our lives. Leave it to Linda to not have it. The drug was an immunization in case she had a reaction to the virus. It could affect her digestively or in the respiratory sense. The drug had to be administered slowly, so the infusion lasted three hours. We only needed to do that one more time in two weeks. The weekly clinic visits were kind of neat. It was like a lung transplant reunion since all the other transplantees are there as well on Tuesday's. We had to go every Tuesday for at least six weeks and possibly up to three months. Of course, they didn't know Linda when they said that. Who knew? We might not need to go after this month. They said she would be in the hospital for a minimum of one week and everyone knows the rest of that story. By the way, the official time of her stay given by the doctor was sixty seven hours, and that's five hours short of three days. I think he was as impressed as much as the rest of us.

This was going to be my last update unless something changed. You could basically say that no news is good news, and everything was going well. Words could not express how much we had appreciated and enjoyed the support and prayers throughout this ordeal. I realized we were not through this yet, and I was not asking everyone to stop thinking and praying for us. I assured folks if I saw them I would have something to say about her progress, but if things continued like they had so far you might see Linda in the Beach to Bay Run.

Chapter Five

Mountain Tops and Valley Lows

I need to go back a few days to the time following the transplant. Linda did very well after the operation, and I was shocked the next morning when I arrived at ICU. Linda was sitting up in bed and immediately asked, "Where have you been?" We had slept in a little, and it was about 9:00 AM. We figured she would still be unconscious, so we all got some much-needed sleep. Boy, how many times can I be wrong? The first day they moved Linda from ICU over to the telemetry unit. I think it was important that the operation was performed before Linda became too ill and lost a lot of her strength. She bounced back quickly and was ready to go home and back to work. We were cleared to leave Saturday morning and actually left about 2:00 PM after all the paperwork was completed. If you consider the first incision was at 2:00 PM Wednesday, this was only seventy-two hours later. New hospital record!

It's amazing how fast Linda recovered. She went back to work in six weeks, and things were back to normal for the most part. Side effects of various drugs were the biggest struggle and prednisone and the anti-rejection drug Gen-Graf were the two biggest problems. The prednisone caused weight gain and a puffy face that always bothered Linda. I reassured her it didn't bother me at all, but this was little comfort to her. The anti-rejection drug ruined her ability to taste foods. This, coupled with an upset stomach, caused her appetite to continue to decline to the point there were only a few foods she would eat. Chocolate pudding and peanut butter and jelly were main stays. There were some mood swings, but I tell you what, for someone that had been through what she had, they were not that bad. I would rather have the mood swings if that's the only way I could have her. I'll never forget what another transplant's husband told me one time, and I have used it several times since. "We'll take them anyway we can get them." Truer words were never spoken.

I guess one of the biggest disappointments about living with a lung transplant is the way it limits your outside activities and your social life. Linda loved working in the yard and working with plants. Lung transplant recipients can never be around dirt or flowers again. Linda's olfactory system became very sensitive, and colognes and perfumes were very repulsive and actually caused her throat to shut and severe choking at times. The unique fact about lung transplant recipients over all others is the lung is exposed to everything in the air. While all other organs are protected in the body from external exposure, lungs get it all. We had to limit our exposure to crowds of any type, which included movie theaters, church, restaurants, and so on. In addition to the threat of colds, flu, other communicable diseases, and with the added inability to tolerate perfumes and colognes, there were very few places we could go. I haven't mentioned the fear of patients, which is they must stay close to their doctor. I guessed if we were to go on another vacation I would have to take Dr. Angel and his family with us.

We had about <u>fifteen months of mostly good times</u>. Compared to what the times would have been without the

Fair Weather Ahead

transplant, I would say they were great times. Around the end of July or the first of August, Linda started getting short of breath. There could have been several things that caused this and of course the most feared was chronic rejection. The testing started and through e-mails, I requested that the prayers begin again.

It was a matter of history how the transplant experience concluded, and I'm confident to this day that the e-mail updates that circulated to literally hundreds of people who prayed for Linda positively affected the outcome. The mixed emotions came from having the need for e-mail updates and knowing that they were effective at generating prayer. I constantly thanked God for friends and family (especially my work family) that showed true concern for Linda and me. It helped to have support. I have to put a plug in for FHR and our insurance as well because without their attitude and assistance, times like these would have been even more difficult. I hear complaints about the cost and the hassle of insurance, and it's a long way from perfect, but what in this world is? The bottom line was our strong faith in God and praying friends kept us going. I will try to summarize, as much as possible, so this doesn't get too long. Most people had heard about Linda's last episode in August. She started getting short of breath and in an attempt to discover the cause, samples of the good lung were needed. In the attempt to get the samples, there was a hole knocked in the lung wall. This was not particularly uncommon because of the procedure involved in obtaining the sample. Long story short, she spent three days in the hospital, came home for two days, and then went back for six more days. Since it included numerous chest tubes, constant labs, x-rays, cat scans, and the usual every three hour blood pressure and temperature check, it was again an unpleasant experience. Between pneumonia, a hole in the lung, and a collapsed lung there were no clear indications of acute rejection. Pulmonary function tests (PFTs) continued to drop and the shortness of breath continued. Pathology reports could not verify rejection, but the doctors all concluded acute rejection was the culprit.

September and half of October had been spent thinning blood to combat blood clotting and changing to a different anti-rejection drug. Linda was directed to have blood drawn every other day and had grown very weary of the constant search for new veins that would allow needles to penetrate. I believe she negotiated for every three days. She had become very frustrated with the inability to perform simple tasks like bending over to pick up another dropped pill. There had been a bright spot in the changing of drugs, and that was the reduction of some side effects. Little comfort to someone that would hardly take an aspirin before and now took two handfuls of pills twice a day.

We were scheduled to go to San Antonio Tuesday the 19th and go through a five-to-seven day infusion therapy that consisted of a daily four-hour infusion of Atgam. This would basically reduce her immune system to zero in an attempt to convince the body not to reject the foreign object, now known as her good lung. CTs had shown that the disease had pretty well destroyed her old lung, and it was just along for the ride now. Everyone's question was why didn't the disease infect the new lung? Don't ask me why; it just didn't. I asked the same thing. I had been assured it would not.

The first question everyone asked was, "What can I do?" I appreciated that and wished there was something they could do besides pray. Linda would be in ICU on the transplant floor at the University of Health Science Center in San Antonio. Visitors would be limited, and they did not allow flowers or plants on that floor. The side effects of the treatment were not pretty by any means. They varied from person to person and included joint pain, nausea, headaches, and on and on. There had been discussions that if the side effects were minimal, we could finish the last two or three days at home. We would have a home health provider come to administer the therapy. Knowing Linda, she would be pushing for that after the first day. Heck knowing her, she would want to go to work in the afternoons.

I had known all my married life that Linda was tough, but I had recently realized she was the toughest person God placed on this green earth. Linda's pride of being a "Texas Woman" drove her to keep pushing and not surrender to the fatigue and overpowering desire to stay in bed, give up all the needle pricks, and skip the chemical ingestion. When I considered my aches and pains of daily life, they paled in comparison, and I'm ashamed I even considered them more than just a minor inconvenience. The patient turned into the encourager. I know Linda would be upset with me if she found out about what I related here. She was a very private individual who shuned the spotlight, and she would interpret this attention as just that. I'll take the heat for the benefit I know this letter will bring.

Writing had become therapeutic to me. I continued to keep everyone posted on Linda's progress. I knew some people desired to do something and suggested cards be sent to the house.

Romans 5:1–5 Peace and Hope

Being therefore justified by faith, we have peace with God through our Lord Jesus Christ;
² through whom also we have had our access by faith into this grace wherein we stand; and we rejoice in hope of the glory of God.
³ And not only so, but we also rejoice in our tribulations: knowing that tribulation worketh stedfastness;
⁴ and stedfastness, approvedness; and approvedness, hope:

⁵ and hope putteth not to shame; because the love of God hath been shed abroad in our hearts through the Holy Spirit which was given unto us.

Actual e-mail responses to Linda's condition:
I will put y'all at the top of my list.

Thanks Keith for keeping me in the loop. . . .Keep the faith.

Please let Linda know that we love her and "As for me and my house, we will be praying for her complete healing." I'll be praying for you as well, I'm sure you feel a little helpless at this point, but know you are and will continue to be a great encourager to her. Yours in Christ,

Our thoughts and prayers are with you and your family. He will see you through this all.

Thanks for the update. I'm sorry to hear there are complications.
However, we will continue to pray for all of you. Your faith is an Inspiration to us. God's plan is perfect.

We completed the transfusions at the house and traveled back to San Antonio on the twelfth of November. Since I was now off on Fridays, we moved our visit days to Friday. It helped that I didn't need to take off on Tuesdays for the doctor visits.

Dr. Angel was in a very somber mood, and we were waiting on some other test results from that morning blood draw. Since the days started early and we could get blood drawn at 6:00 AM, we would leave Corpus Christi at 4:00 AM or so. So that Linda could eat as soon as the blood was drawn, we tried to be the first in line. We would then be waiting on the x-ray department to open at 7:00 AM and from there to the PFT lab and wait on them to open at 7:30 AM. We would go to the eighth floor for the doctor's visit and usually waited till 10:00 AM for that. Some days when things were not going well at the hospital we would wait until after lunch. It often made for long days.

Dr. Angel came into the room about noon. I could tell he didn't want to be there. I had learned his body language, and I knew this wasn't good. He said the lung was in rejection and that there was nothing else that could be done. Of course, our first question was, "Can we get another transplant?" He said that they had been discussing it, but the board had said no. It seems their thinking was that why give someone a second chance when there are people out there waiting to get their first one. He said not to give up because he hadn't given up.

So, we made yet another long trip back to Corpus Christi without much conversation. During those times Linda would be so fatigued that she would sleep all the way home. It was hard enough just to breathe, but when you added in all the activity on our visit days, it was just too much. Now, sleeping most of the time on road trips had become the norm.

Chapter Six

God of Second Chances

*B*y November 19, 2004, we were playing the waiting game again. We talked to Dr. Angel at our visit on the nineteenth. He said they still were not all in agreement about second transplants but not to give up. He said one of his arguments included the fact that Linda had done everything correctly and followed all directions to make this a successful transplant. He said the board and everyone else in the University of Texas Health and Science Center were well aware of Linda and her commitment to make it work. That could be a deciding factor, but so far a decision had not been made.

Linda's PFTs continued to fall, and I could see where things were digressing quickly. I really started to think she wouldn't make it to the end of the year. She was struggling to do anything on her own and as much as she wanted to finish a project, she was operating on the spirit is willing but the body is weak rationale. We were praying that God would see it in His will to grant the second transplant, but if it wasn't, we would accept that as well.

On November 23, 2004, we received a great birthday present for Linda (12/1) when Dr. Angel called to let us

Fair Weather Ahead

know that the board had agreed to give Linda another lung. Needless to say, it was a great Thanksgiving, full of thanks. We traveled to San Antonio to get all the preliminary testing started on December 9th. It was a lot easier this time since we knew where everything was and what to expect. It was kind of like visiting all of our old friends.

All the tests went well, and we were ready to go except for the heart catheter. They usually wait until it's closer to the transplant. We were still waiting to hear from the insurance company that all was good to go and officially be placed on the list. So we returned home to wait—some more!

On December 15, 2004, we received the call that all was good, and we were on the organ list and needed to go to San Antonio for the heart catheter. We arrived early Thursday morning, and there was some confusion about whether Linda was supposed to take her Coumadin (blood thinner) or not. We knew the normal procedure was not to take it, but we had been having so much trouble with blood clots that the doctor performing the procedure said to stay on it. When we arrived they asked if she had taken the Coumadin and of course we had to say she had. There was a lot of discussion about postponing the procedure, but timing was becoming critical. The decision was made to proceed.

Linda completed the procedure without any problems, and the doctor said everything looked good; the transplant could proceed. The process involved an incision in the main artery in her leg. They ran a camera with instruments to measure the capacity of the heart and make sure it was strong enough to handle the transplant operation. I'm sure they didn't want to waste an organ on someone with a heart that would not hold up.

Linda was resting in the recovery room, which was comprised of about ten beds separated only with curtains. While we were sitting there waiting for them to give us the word we could go home, we picked out our lunch stop. They still had all the monitoring equipment hooked up, and I was always watching the numbers and the little lines that ran across the screens. I saw the blood pressure start to drop and within a few seconds it became terribly low. I stood up and raised the sheet that was over her legs, and the bed was soaked in blood. The incision had come open, and I felt I was to blame. Since they had not let Linda eat anything that morning, she was hungry. I dug around in our back pack emergency kit that had just about everything except the kitchen sink in it. I found some crackers and offered them to her. She was eating one and choked on it and was coughing. That is what opened the incision, and she was bleeding out as the artery was pumping straight to the bed.

I hollered for a nurse, and I was glad one of the male nurses showed up. He immediately jumped on the incision with both hands and with all his weight held the incision closed. He had his shoulders hunched up and was applying as much of his body weight as he could. He stopped the bleeding almost immediately and applied the pressure for an hour and twenty minutes. It was an amazing display of human strength and determination. He had sweat rolling off his head and once he felt like it was safe to let go he fell slumped into a chair.

So, naturally they wouldn't let us leave. It was about 7:00 that evening before they had a bed for Linda to check into. I sat there for quite some time thinking how I had messed this up and we could be at home, but then something came to me. What if we had been half way between San Antonio and Corpus Christi and we hit a bump or she coughed and the incision opened up there? She would most likely have bled out and died on the shoulder of the road. I was thankful for the cracker.

December 16, 2004, we returned home to play the waiting game once again. We hadn't decorated for any holidays in quite some time. I'm not even sure we knew it was a holiday. Things were not getting any better, and I could see that we had reached the point that something needed to happen fast. I figured if there were no more emergencies or catastrophes that Linda wouldn't make it through January.

On Thursday, December 23, 2004, we received the call about 2:00 PM to be in San Antonio that afternoon. Since it wasn't in the middle of the night, it seemed unusual. Everything seemed to always happen in the middle of the night, weekends, or holidays. One out of three is not bad. We headed to San Antonio and arrived after 5:00 PM. When you try to check in after the front desk is closed you have to check in through the emergency room. I don't know if you have ever been to the emergency room at The University of Texas Health and Science Center but it is the county hospital. There were lots of people packed in the waiting room, and I wasn't about to take Linda in there. I told the nurse Linda was a transplant patient and she couldn't sit out in the waiting room. She said okay, and we headed down the hall to a room. I walked in and took one glance at the situation and said, "No, she's not coming in here either." There were about twenty beds all separated by curtains. I said that she couldn't be in there with all those sick people. The nurse thought a minute and said, "You're right!" We headed back down the hall and they found her a private room. We both fell asleep for about an hour before someone showed up.

We headed upstairs and started all the blood work. It was after midnight before we heard that we should be getting an organ any minute.

On December 24, 2004, the miracles of Christmas occurred. We headed to the operating room about 10:00 AM on Christmas Eve. What a Christmas present for us, but Linda couldn't help but think about how terrible of a Christmas it was for the donor family. She had never really settled the issue of the first donor and the cost it had to their family. I headed to the waiting room where there was one other

God Of Second Chances

man. We struck up a conversation, and I soon found out his wife would be receiving the other lung from the donor. We decided we were somehow in-laws. He and his wife were both retired military, and she had IPF same as Linda. This was her first transplant. We had a lot to talk about so the time went by pretty fast. The nurse came out and told me when they were starting to sew in the new lung, and before I knew it, they said that if I wanted to see her, I would need to go to the twelfth floor. She did it again!

I met with the surgeon afterwards, and I noticed something wasn't quite right. He started to say something about the connection, but half way through he decided not to. Then, it was more about what he didn't say than what he said. I knew something wasn't right, and it had to do with the area between the new lung and where it attached. This would end up causing us lots of complications in 2005 and eventually contribute to an unsuccessful (at least long term) transplant.

There was lots of excitement about the snow that had covered the ground south of San Antonio. There was just a dusting there at the hospital but the further south you went the deeper the snow and higher the excitement. Everyone was out playing in the snow, and we were just as happy to be where we were, enjoying our own Christmas blessing. We went home Tuesday, December 28 without concerns of records or anything else. I don't think either one of us was really comfortable with this transplant from the beginning. We were just happy to get an extension. Praise God!

As we pulled on to the freeway I phoned Joan, my sister, to tell her we were headed home. She told me then that mama was in the hospital and not expected to make it through the night. Since we had enough to deal with, she had been withholding the information about mama. For many reasons, it was a quiet ride home. Mom had been out of touch with this world for some years, and we knew this day would come soon.

Mary Frances Lawrence passed away in the early hours of Wednesday December 29, 2004 at the age of ninety years. Linda was heartbroken since she and mom had a great relationship. Linda was equally upset because she couldn't attend the funeral.

Chapter Seven

Intestinal Fortitude Defined

On Sunday, March 6, 2005, the morning routine started at 6:30. The daily pills were laid out and breakfast was being prepared. Linda was sitting up in bed and had requested cereal. The menu didn't change that much. It was usually oatmeal or some type of cereal. She used to order toast a lot, but it was getting more difficult to eat as her breathing was becoming worse. We all experience a small sensation of this when we have a head cold. The cereal was delivered, and she tried to take a bite but couldn't get it down. It was obvious that things were worse.

She tried several times, and we turned the oxygen up full blast, and she rested between bite attempts. Finally, she looked at me and said we have to go to the hospital. She could not catch her breath. I dialed 911.

I loved the fire fighters and all the paramedics. Those guys got there so fast, and when the Calvary came, they came in force. They really made us feel good when they walked in the door.

Since the meds changed all the time, we had all Linda's meds on the computer and as soon as I dialed 911, I pushed print.

Fair Weather Ahead

I called my sister and brother and headed to the hospital. They had her in ICU but really didn't know what to do with her. Since transplant patients are so unique, the treatment is totally different. Corpus Christi doesn't see that many transplant patients. They immediately placed a call to San Antonio and had Dr. Angel and Dr. Palaez on the phone. Her blood pressure was nonexistent. I remember one time they couldn't get it to read on the blood pressure cuff. Finally, they found a 70 over 25. They administered Dopamine and her blood pressure started racing and both blood pressure numbers were over 190. They began chasing the high blood pressure and the low blood pressure at the same time. It was just like a roller coaster, but the ride was no fun.

They immediately started talking about transferring her to San Antonio. They had to stabilize her first, and that wasn't going to be easy. They started calling a medical transfer plane, but they could not fill the crew. There were no pilots available. This went on all morning until finally they decide to use Halo Flight helicopters. One problem was Halo Flight only flies out of Memorial, and we were at Spohn Shoreline. They (Corpus and San Antonio) finally decided to make the move around 2:30 that afternoon. Dr. Angel was about to go crazy because they couldn't get her to San Antonio.

The flight crew from Halo Flight showed up to start getting her ready for the ambulance ride to Memorial Hospital. I said I would meet them in San Antonio. I ran by the house and grabbed a couple of clean shorts and headed north. I won't discuss my driving habits but I did have my flashers on. I saw one highway patrol just out of San Antonio and I watched him to see if he was going to turn around, but it looked like he didn't even see me. The helicopter beat me by twenty minutes.

When I arrived at the ICU they already had Linda hooked up and working on her.

Intestinal Fortitude Defined

Dr. Angel and Dr. Palaez were there. Dr. Angel said if her blood gases didn't improve pretty quick, he would intubate her. Linda was arguing that she didn't need it, just a mask with some oxygen. Dr. Angel said twenty minutes was all he would give her and walked out. He came back in ten minutes and had her intubated. This started the longest ten days of my life.

I wasn't ready for what happened next. They told me Linda was in septic shock. I had no idea what it meant, but the word septic, used in any situation, couldn't be good. I hung around the waiting room with strangers who soon became friends. There is another society that forms in the waiting rooms of doctors' offices and hospitals, especially in the transplant world. You are constantly spending hours upon hours with each other waiting for the ICU door to open to learn some type of information about your loved one. It gets pretty hectic.

Kenda, John, and Ethan arrived, and we all stayed in a local motel. Kenda and I seemed to sleep very little, especially early in the morning. We would wake up about 4:00 AM and sneak out to the truck where we prayed until daylight in the hospital parking lot. This was a dramatic turning point in the relationship between Kenda and me. There is not a bigger blessing in the world than when one of your children comes back at a real time of need and becomes your spiritual leader. The prayers in the cab of that truck on those mornings were unbelievable. I will never forget trying to pray, "Your will be done," and could not get the words out. I wanted my will, and that was for Linda to get up and walk out. I was afraid if I gave God an option, He would take her home. Finally, after several mornings and sticking on the words that would not come out of my mouth, I said them: "God I just ask that Your will be done." I don't know what Kenda felt, but I thought the truck was shaking. It was as if a huge load had been lifted from my shoulders. I started bawling like a baby (this was not an unusual event).

We found out on Monday that Linda's kidneys were failing. There had been no urine output, and that wasn't good. I remember thinking this was it. I returned to the motel room where Joan and Charles were staying, and they asked what was wrong when I walked in. I just broke down and said this was it. I figured when the organs started shutting down that it was over.

They hooked Linda up to the kidney dialysis machine Tuesday night. She was bloating so badly that the IV needles would push out. I had no idea the human body could get so big without the skin tearing. It was very difficult to go into the room with her. I remember looking at the tubes running to the dialysis machine and thinking how cold it was making her. She would get cold very quickly anyway, and with the tubes hanging in the air, I thought about it being like a refrigerant system. I would cover her every time I came in, but the nurses would leave the covers off when they worked on her.

Dr. Angel and Dr. Palez came to the waiting room on Wednesday. I knew the news wasn't going to be good. They said Linda had a 50/50 chance of making it, a coin toss. She was very sick, and sometimes when patients got like this, they would make it, and sometimes they wouldn't. He said it would be best for me to go home. I hadn't thought of that.

I called everyone that was staying in town and told them to all go home. I would be leaving for Corpus Christi in a little while myself. That wasn't easy at all. I remember driving and just questioning over and over again if I knew what I was doing. How could I just leave her lying up there and not even be in the same town? It was tearing my guts out. I don't know how one person can cry so many tears. I stopped at the rest area on the way back (it's half way between the hospital and our house). I sat out there on the picnic table and

Intestinal Fortitude Defined

paced the sidewalk for an hour trying to decide to go north or south. I finally headed south.

I called Mark when I reached Edroy and asked if he would come to the house. I didn't think about it being Wednesday night and how he already had obligations. He showed up, and we prayed, or he prayed and I cried. I remember thinking that I didn't have enough faith to get through this. I didn't, but God did, and He gave it to me.

I went to work sometime Thursday just to catch up on the e-mails and anything else that needed my attention. My body was there, but my mind was in San Antonio. I could call the ICU nurse's station anytime and did frequently. Nothing changed from one call to the next, but it was good just to hear the nurse's voices. I really had some good nurses, and we even spent some time crying together while I was there. I made it to about 2:00 that afternoon and couldn't stand it any longer. I jumped in the truck and drove to San Antonio. I walked in the ICU, took one look at Linda, and stayed about ten minutes. I talked to a couple of nurses and discovered there was no change. I turned around and drove back to Corpus Christi. I remember I wasn't there long, because my parking time hadn't exceeded the first thirty minutes.

It seemed that things started turning a little better by the weekend. I managed to hold out until Saturday to go back to San Antonio and stay the weekend. She was still being supported by all the machines and intubated but there were some life signs that kept them from placing a permanent dialysis port in her side. She started making tiny bits of urine, and we all watched that bag like it was the Super Bowl. I urged her to make some urine. She would kill me if she knew I said that.

It seemed as if there was no end to the hurdles that kept popping up while Linda made baby steps out of her coma. I waited for ten days to hear the words "the pneumonia broke." The pneumonia had a death grip on Linda that the doctors

Fair Weather Ahead

had warned me could go south any minute. If the pneumonia tipped any in the wrong direction, the battle would be over. You can imagine how I waited for the words "it broke."

Finally an x-ray indicated the pneumonia looked a little better in the upper lobe of the lung. Hallelujah, we're out of the woods. Well, not exactly. The kidneys probably wouldn't come back, and Linda had been on the dialysis machine through the main pic in her left groin. The doctors were concerned with infection and decided to install the permanent port in her right shoulder. The lack of oxygen had caused permanent failure, and she would be required to have dialysis for the rest of her life. Well, I knew she wasn't going to like that, so I told her and God the kidneys needed to start functioning. The day the doctors came in to install the dock, the doctor looked down at the bag on the side of the bed and said, "Well, look at that!" She had made a small amount of urine in the past couple of hours, and he decided to wait till tomorrow. Tomorrow came and the kidneys were working better. They became better every day until they were fully functioning, and the dock wasn't necessary. Hallelujah, we're out of the woods! Well, not exactly.

I don't remember exactly how the conversation went, but I can tell you this: Dr. Palaze wasn't very good at giving bad news. I was telling him how we must be past the crisis because the white blood cells were up where they belonged, the kidneys were working, and the pneumonia had shown signs of breaking. Usually, he wouldn't look straight at me when he had bad news, and I could tell since he was looking somewhere else in the room that the bad news was coming. He wanted to do a CT; a CT what for? There could be brain damage. This was a totally new idea to me. I never considered that because of the lack of oxygen Linda could have brain damage. It really upset me because I knew Linda would not want to be in a vegetative state. There just happen to be a high profile case going on in the country at the same time,

Intestinal Fortitude Defined

and I couldn't imagine having to deal with the issues that family dealt with while the entire world watched. However, the CT was clear, more answered prayer.

Just as important, due to all of the medications, the pneumonia, and just all the lung had been through, there was a question about the condition of the lung. It wasn't sixty days ago the lung resided in another person. I don't think the doctors were very optimistic that the organ would take all the abuse and still work. If anyone doubts the power of prayer, then they need to consider this case. All of Linda's organs had shut down from lack of oxygen, and she had been given very large doses of steroids, which destroyed muscle mass. Don't forget the heart is a muscle. Even after all that had happened, every organ seemed to have come back to its previous state, but it would take some time to really know the condition of the lung. Early PFTs seemed to indicate there would be no lasting damage. I guess a person could say, "She sure is lucky!" or "Those doctors are really good!" How about, "That new technology is something else!" Having lived the whole thing, I would say without a doubt the doctors were really good and the technology was great, but most of all, "Our God is an awesome God!"

When you see the big picture of this experience and realize how all the pieces fit together, one would have to agree it was more than coincidence or luck that made everything work out the way it did. I think everyone involved in the experience is closer to God today than they were when this journey started.

I returned home Sunday night and was feeling better. We were not out of the woods, but things looked so much better now. They called Monday night and said they were thinking about taking her off dialysis Tuesday. I left for San Antonio about 4:00 Tuesday morning.

I didn't think I would ever be so glad to see someone's kidneys working. There were more ounces of urine this hour

Fair Weather Ahead

than the last and the amount seemed to be increasing with each passing hour. Linda's swelling had gone down, and she seemed to be breathing easier, even though she was still on the ventilator. Dr. Angel said it looked like she would make it after all, and if today was as good as yesterday, we could remove all the support the next day. It turns out the dialysis machine came off that afternoon.

Early Wednesday morning, they removed the ventilator and the first words she spoke when I walked in were, "Where is Ethan?" I was thrilled and told her not to worry; he was downstairs in the lobby. It's hard to explain how it feels to communicate with someone again after ten days of silence. I often wondered if I would ever converse with her again this side of heaven.

I have been told that the muscles start to atrophy after only three days of inactivity. I was shocked at how much muscle control Linda had lost. She was only able to move her little finger on her left hand. That was it! She couldn't move her legs or arms or even raise her head. The inactivity coupled with the strong medications she had been subjected to had totally disabled her. We found out the meds would cause her hair to fall out, but that was minor at that point. Since she was back with us, the rest didn't matter.

The next big step was the laborious task of rehab. Anyone who knew Linda knew that she would not like to be spoon fed and waited on for every little thing. It was very exasperating for her, but you would have never known by the way she treated everyone. We had great physical and occupational therapists who seemed to connect with Linda as soon as they walked in the door. She would get frustrated, but I think they saw her drive to get back her strength, and they had to have recognized a fighter when they saw her. The steps back were small and moved extremely slowly for Linda. She urged them to do two-a-days so she could return sooner. We eventually did move to two-a-days after I learned how to perform

Intestinal Fortitude Defined

the exercises. The therapists did not work on weekends, so I took over the rehab task on Saturdays and Sundays. Even though I might have chosen a different method, it presented another opportunity for us to spend quality time together. Seeing her work so hard and the daily progression encouraged me.

With the help of two physical therapists, one on each side, Linda walked three feet on Thursday. On Friday, we placed two chairs five feet apart, and she walked back and forth four times with a small break at each chair. Later that same afternoon, Dr. Angel came by, our hero, and Linda had to show off for him. She made it to the chair and decided not to stop. Her knees buckled about one step from the home chair. She was very disappointed and apologetic that she didn't make it, but Dr. Angel and his entourage were very impressed. She was medically stable and ready to be move on to the next step (get it?). We waited for a bed to open up at Methodist Specialty and Transplant Hospital, which is the intermediate rehab facility that would build Linda's strength. It would prepare her to go to a full-blown rehab unit or maybe even go to the house. I toured the facility Saturday. It is a thirty- bed unit that specializes in patients who are on ventilators or have otherwise been in a coma for a length of time. After eight weeks, two days, and twenty-three-and-a-half hours, it was very exciting to walk out of University Hospital. The length of stay depended on how Linda progressed, but knowing her and the way she would work to get out, it would be as soon as possible. After visiting with her physical therapist at University Hospital, she was amazed by the progress Linda had made in the week before we moved to Methodist Specialty and Transplant Hospital. She figured Linda had made about three weeks' progress in one week.

When we entered Methodist Specialty and Transplant Hospital, it was very intense. Lots of questions and examinations took place. Linda was a little apprehensive because now there were all new nurses and doctors. When we discovered that the pulmonary doctor had trained under Dr. Angel and they were friends, our comfort level increased.

On the rehab floor, they can be very discouraging sometimes, especially for someone who thinks she is not sick. There are great stories about recovery and comebacks but it's often hard to live in that atmosphere on a daily basis. Linda started asking to get out the first day we were there. We were told it would be thirty days of rehab and Linda said, "I don't think so!" She was walking some with the walker, and when we would do one lap around the halls, she would want to do two. I would come in the room, and she would be lifting her legs or arms, working out. She wasn't staying thirty days.

Since that Sunday morning, eight weeks had passed since we started this latest adventure. One reason we moved to the Methodist Hospital was the doctors wanted Linda off the twelfth floor, which was where all the transplant patients resided when they visited the hospital. Since the area was very dangerous due to viruses and bugs being passed around, Linda had been placed in seclusion on the floor.

When I left San Antonio Sunday, Linda's instructions to me were to return Thursday night April 28, 2005, because we would go home Friday. Not wanting to upset the apple cart or Linda, I agreed, not sure I really believed it would happen. Proved my ignorance again! Monday, she called and said she had talked to Dr. Birch, and he didn't see a problem with her leaving, but he wasn't going to be here, so it would be up to the doctor on duty. A long story short, she was leaving the hospital and headed home regardless of anyone's opinion. Medically, she was stable, and there were no issues with her lung or health. Some believed she needed more rehab, and one social worker I talked to just couldn't imagine her leaving. I told her she knew Linda's room number, so she could just get right down there and tell her that. It was hard

Intestinal Fortitude Defined

for me to believe she needed much more rehab if six doctors, eight nurses and three social workers couldn't keep her there. Heck, I don't think a herd of wild horses could have held her back. We had been waiting for this day a long time and excited didn't quite explain how we felt. Linda's spirits were high, and she was working extra hard with the rehab, and I didn't see her slowing down at the house. She was working out with three-pound weights and walking, with a walker, over 660 feet per day. Not all at one time, but in three different sessions per day. Since the return date moved up so quickly, my family and friends had quite a surprise planned for her return and had been scrambling to complete their plans.

We left after two weeks with a clear medical discharge, but that was only because Linda was determined to leave with or without the paper work. We did wheel her to the truck in a wheel chair, but she stood up and climbed in almost by herself. We were headed home, and it felt great. I wasn't sure if I would make that trip to Corpus Christi alone or with her, but there we were going home and we were together again after ten weeks.

Leaving Methodist Specialty and Transplant Hospital

Chapter Eight

Giving Thanks, Renewing Commitments, and Goals Reached

*I*n June of 2005, I set out to write thank you notes and quickly realized I would need to write hundreds of them if I tried to address each group. Not that I wouldn't, but I probably couldn't since there are so many people out there to thank, and I don't even know who they all were. Thanks to the World Wide Web, the request for prayer and the sharing of Linda's situation had spread around the world. I heard about churches and individuals that were concerned and prayed for Linda that I had never met or even knew for sure how they were connected. The support had been amazing. Not that I ever doubted everyone's concern, but the fact everyone would be so supportive was reassuring.

I have to start out with our home church, Oak Ridge Baptist Church. The phone calls, the cards, and the meals were great and came just at the right time. It was no accident that I crossed paths with these fine people when I needed them most. Linda, Kenda, and I thought about the next one for a long time. We received a card each week signed by the

Giving Thanks, Renewing Commitments, And Goals Reached

Wednesday Night Faithful at Pruitt Baptist Church in Van, Texas. We tried to tie the connection to cousins, uncles, and any other family member we could imagine. We even looked at a map to see where in the world Van, Texas is located. We read all the names on the cards each Wednesday and didn't recognize any of them. Then one day, when a work acquaintance and I discussed Linda's condition, she mentioned her dad called every Wednesday morning for an update on Linda. Then, she mentioned his church prayed for Linda every Wednesday. I asked if they happened to be in Van, Texas and she said yes. The mystery was solved. Thanks for your faithfulness in lifting us up in your prayers.

I can't even imagine how to collect all the names of groups that supported us in prayer. There were deacon groups, Sunday school classes, home Bible studies, other individuals, and the list goes on and on. I hesitate to try and list names of churches that have responded because I know I will leave some out, but it's important to mention those I can think of. They are Gateway Baptist Church, Riverwood Baptist Church, Annaville Baptist, Grace United Methodist, First United Methodist Church Aransas Pass, St. John Baptist Church, Our Lady of Guadalupe, Calvary Chapels all over the United States, and on and on. I had been told of so many stories of special prayers in just about every kind of gathering you can imagine. One of my favorites was about a man and his son who went to the missions in Goliad and lifted special prayers for Linda. I had heard about people in California, North Dakota, North Carolina, Kansas, and even Iraq praying for Linda. It was really overwhelming!

The number of cards that we received was astounding. We could have wall papered Linda's room with the cards from people. There were so many thoughtful cards that lifted our spirits each time we opened them and read the words sent from you to us. If you sent a card, thanks.

Fair Weather Ahead

This next part is even harder to put into words. I don't understand how God plans our lives or how he determines which obstacles He allows each of us to encounter. I'm sure that some experiences are caused by our own choices, but God has a plan for each of us. I don't know how he decides who gets ninety years on this earth and some only get weeks. I do believe we are to experience struggles and conflicts so we can grow. A tree that never encounters the wind of everyday life will blow over at the first sign of real wind that eventually comes along. The main thing is we must continue to praise God in all things. All things include the seemingly impossible struggles we live through.

Life has been explained as many things, but in reality it is just a preparation for our real life, which comes next. We each have an appointment with physical death that can't be avoided. I have always believed that if your number is up, there is nothing you can do. I'm wondering now if that's entirely true. If God didn't intend for Linda to die during this last experience, then he intended her to get within fractions of an inch of doing so. I'm not sure if the praying prevented her from dying or if the close call was to get us to pray. Either way we all were forced to realize we have nothing to combat death except Jesus Christ.

I made a comment after Linda's first transplant that this experience had brought me back into a closer relationship with God. Linda's comment was, "I'm glad I was here to go through it for you." There was a clear tone of sarcasm in her voice. I can't imagine why some people seem to go through more than others. I look at parents and grandparents, a new perspective for me, who have lost children and think how much worse their pain is than ours. I see people who have suffered injuries that have taken away their freedom to function in everyday life for the rest of their lives and can only thank God for my health. But the reality was, Linda had been through so much more than most people will ever know. I haven't come close to the pain, suffering, setbacks, or illness that Linda had seen, but there was a certain amount of pain and suffering that a spouse endures with a soul mate.

I have said all of this to say I don't know how we would have made it through all of this had it not been for the support that God sent our way. There were so many good things that had come out of this roller coaster ride of emotions, and it might take years for all of them to be realized. Because of all of this, I had a new closer relationship with Linda and Kenda. You can't help but admire Linda even more for her "never give up" attitude. Kenda's strong faith in God and ability to totally submit to Him helped me to do so as well. There were nights that seemed to be the darkest, and God would have someone call me at just the right moment. The cards in the mailbox, the e-mails of encouragement, and just the never-ending words of comfort and support made it all bearable. "Thank you" falls so short of what I want to say, but I don't know what the words are that I can convey what I feel to both those of you I know and those that I don't. Someday when I see you in heaven I can really thank you.

I might have waited too long to capture the details, but it was mid-August and I'm going to relate the incidents and events associated with one of the most beautiful days in our combined life. June 18, 2005, Linda and I renewed our wedding vows. It was a great day, and I hope I can capture the meaning for each of us as the main participants but also the emotions, significance, and heartfelt connection of all of those in attendance.

I have to go back to mid-March. Linda had been in a comma for two weeks, hooked up to life support. The doctors had said it was a coin flip if she would make it or not. We had been through so many close calls and touchy situations since 1999, but this was more real than all of the others combined. Even the transplants themselves were not as traumatic.

Fair Weather Ahead

I had had a helpless feeling since this ordeal started, but now it was worse than ever. I realized how few times I said, "I love you." I just wanted to hear her voice one more time. I just wanted to have a conversation with her about anything and everything. I would go into her room amidst the humming of the kidney dialysis machine and the rhythmic beat of the ventilator and talk to her as if nothing was wrong. I had heard stories of people in comas being able to hear and comprehend conversation. I tried to tell her what had happened in our family that day and any other news I thought might interest her. I'll never forget struggling with the news that the Spurs had traded Malik Rose to the Nicks. Malik was one of her favorite players, and I knew it would upset her. Finally after about a week, I told her. Turns out she didn't hear a thing. I can't explain the tightness in my chest and the burning desire I had just for her to acknowledge my presence. I would have settled for an eyebrow raise, wink, or any type of response. There was none.

Those days were terrible as I watched her lie right there at arm's length, yet she was so far away. I remember worrying that she would be cold because the tubes transporting blood back and forth to the dialysis machine were just hanging in the air. She would get cold at home with simple infusions at room temp. They assured me she couldn't feel a thing, but I covered her up anyway every time I went in there.

I know people say at that last moment, their life passes right before their eyes. I believed our life together was passing right before my eyes. I recalled all kinds of silly things that we had done together and wondered how we lived through some of them. I constantly thought of things she would be saying. "It would be better to turn from that lane," or "You didn't tighten the lid on the ketchup," and many others. There was a time I might have thought (to myself) "quit nagging," but not now. I would have loved to hear some nagging. Although I don't believe Linda is a nagger, I'm just a

Giving Thanks, Renewing Commitments, And Goals Reached

slow learner! It took me ten years to learn to raise the seat and another ten too not leave it up.

I knew Linda was a fighter, and there were literally hundreds, if not a thousand people praying for Linda. I still spent every waking hour wondering if I would get the chance to say the words from my heart I now so desperately needed to verbalize. There were times I would not allow those words out, but now they were choking me. That might explain the constant tightness in my heart; it was from crowding.

In my times of stress, the keyboard brought me the most relief. Even at work when I got uptight about an issue or a situation I sat down and typed out my thoughts, feelings, and suggestions. Often I would hit the delete button when I was finished, but it really cleared my head and offered an avenue to vent. This time was no different. I started writing down what I wanted to say, and before I knew it, I was proposing to her all over again. That's when I realized I wanted to show everyone that I loved Linda more than anything in the world. I had to admit I thought it might give her some incentive to keep fighting to get through this. Turns out she already had plenty of incentive for that.

Two weeks passed without any type of communication from her. Finally, on a Saturday she opened her eyes. She couldn't talk because she was still on the ventilator . They removed the ventilator and when I walked in Sunday morning the first words she mouthed without any sound were, "Where is Ethan?" I said, "Hey, what am I, chopped liver?"

So she could communicate better and also fully understand what I meant. I waited another week before I read her the letter I had written.

The longer I thought about it, the better it sounded. I could imagine how Linda and Kenda would be planning and plotting all the details and hopefully get excited about the idea. I could imagine the smallest detail getting discussed and how they would spend hours deciding how and what to do. I wasn't disappointed. The excitement built with each phone call, and then the weekend came.

Here is the invitation to the renewing ceremony:

With much Joy, Jubilation and Celebration we invite you to join us as we renew our vows of commitment to each other.

Please join us on Saturday, June 18, 2005, at 5:00 O'Clock at Colonial Hills United Methodist Church located at 5247 Vance Jackson Rd, San Antonio Linda and Keith respectfully request your attendance in this celebration. After 34 years of marriage together God has given us the opportunity to publicly affirm, to Him in your presence, that His plan is perfect. Due to Linda's sensitive sense of smell please do not wear any perfume or aftershave.

No gifts please your presence is gifting enough. Scrubs welcome. Refreshments to follow

I was concerned, and I knew Dr. Angel wondered if she would be in the hospital that weekend or not. She had been struggling with a cough and was getting in that run-down state again. She was at the clinic Tuesday, and they gave her some high-powered medications to boost her red blood cells and give her some energy. These drugs always brought on flu-like symptoms and tended to drag her down for two or three days. There wasn't any way that she was missing this event!

Friday, Colby, Kenda, John, Ethan, Linda, and I stayed in the Hearth Inn in San Antonio. Linda had an appointment at a local beauty shop to fix her scarf in an African fashion.

Giving Thanks, Renewing Commitments, And Goals Reached

Although it was growing back, Linda didn't have much hair and needed a little help. She and Kenda didn't know I had scheduled a massage, nails, and makeup for both of them. Kenda decide she didn't want the massage but would take the full hair deal and nails instead. Unfortunately the massage was upstairs, and Linda couldn't make it up the stairs, but she had her nails and hair done. They treated her great, and she really enjoyed it. She was a beautiful bride.

With the hospital staff in mind, we held the ceremony at the Oak Hills Methodist Church in San Antonio. To make it easier for anyone working that day or night to attend, scrubs were welcomed. Several of the physical therapists attended as well as the pulmonary function testing technician. A good number of people from Corpus Christi, as well as San Antonio, attended. We had a couple from Houston fly in, and Dr. Angel and his family made it.

Kenda and Linda had gathered up childhood pictures and some of the items from the first wedding and displayed them on a table in the foyer of the church. The colors were purple, of course, and while everything was simple, it was simply beautiful. Colby stole the show with his dress white Navy uniform. Linda had asked him to dress in it, but he had all kinds of excuses why he couldn't. I started looking for him to get the ceremony started and he was nowhere to be found. Then, he showed up out of nowhere with a clean shave and wearing those bright dress whites. Linda was blown away.

Linda & Colby

Both of us had written our own vows, and Mark Miller, our pastor, had written some vows for us as well. I don't believe there was a dry eye in the house. The fact that Linda was able to stand there that day and once again affirm her love for me and I for her was a blessing from God. I know that each person in that church on that day had a connection with both of us that passed all human understanding. It was admiration, respect, hope, but most of all love that brought us all together. There could have been no better way to acknowledge how we all felt than to celebrate the life of two people spent together as God intended. Living life, struggling together, celebrating together, raising a family, and now looking back confirming it was all worth it. We were happiest because we had been through it all as one.

Giving Thanks, Renewing Commitments, And Goals Reached

Linda's Vows:

Who knew. . . .
When we met at 18 we'd still be together today
You'd be my protector, my encourager and my hero.
I'd be treated like a princess, with you waiting on me hand and foot!
You'd have to deal with so much sickness.
But you have certainly been my "better" during my "worse."
God knew when he made us partners.
Thank you for standing by me.

My Vows:

Almost 36 years ago when the most beautiful girl I had ever seen in my life walked into my government class I had no idea that the rest of my life would be so affected. I was so naïve; I actually thought I had a chance to get you to go on a date with me and from that day to today all my energy has been spent trying to impress you. Little did I know God arranged this encounter, and neither one of us could imagine what lay ahead. We did go on that first date to a football game, and as they say, the rest is history.

You have given me the fullest life, one that I couldn't have imagined. You convinced me that we needed to have a family and gave me two of my greatest accomplishments in life, Colby and Kenda. Now it has grown to include John and Ethan. God knew what it would take to make me happy and be fulfilled, and he sent that happiness and fulfillment to me through you.

Looking back I now see all the "for better or worse" and realize we enjoyed each other as much, if not more, in the worse as in the better. We learned the most about each other during the worse times, and during those times we really became one. I believe that's why God put us together: because He knew that together we made a person that could handle the worse. I have so many good memories that I cherish, and often they come back to me with much joy. This latest battle with a terrible disease has taught me how much and how deeply I really love you. I wouldn't wish this disease on my worst enemy, but it has slowed us down to realize what it is we really mean to each other. I think we all have a tendency to become complacent and apathetic, taking relationships for granted in the good times and not really cherishing each other, as God intended.

We have been fortunate to watch those that have gone and go before us. Mom and Dad showed us all how to be one. My Dad showed me how to take care of my wife. My sister and brother showed us that the tough time in a marriage doesn't mean give up. We thank you all for the examples.

But I have to thank you for teaching me what a soul mate is. I have seen you hurt worse than I did when I was in pain. I witnessed you be the happiest you could possibly be just because I was happy. You supported and encouraged me, and when it seemed the whole world was after me, you comforted and convinced me we could get through whatever it was that we faced. You are my soul mate.

This time my words have much more meaning, and I understand what true commitment to someone is. So, as I consider my vows today I have to at least say, "I pledge thee my troth" as a repeat of our first vows. First time I said those words I wasn't even sure what it meant, but you have taught me the true meaning. I have to say I will take you again for "better or worse" because now I know we are better "together" in the worse.

You know that I believe a person's actions speak louder than their words. Let my actions today speak for me to say,

"If I had it all to do over again, I would, and today I am doing it all over again."

I love You and I want to spend whatever time we have remaining just enjoying your company, cherishing you, and standing together to face whatever is next because I know the three of us can handle anything. I love you more than you will ever know.

Dr. Angel and his family were there, and this was a tremendous thrill for Linda. I remember Dr. Angel saying what an effort it took for Linda to be there and appear as if nothing was wrong. I think he and I were the only two that really understood what she had to do to be there.

Keith and the beautiful bride, again

Fair Weather Ahead

The wedding party. Joan, Charlotte, Pastor Mark, Kenda, Linda, Keith, Colby, John, JW, Charles (Hoot)

Kissing the bride again

Giving Thanks, Renewing Commitments, And Goals Reached

Linda & Dr. Angel our hero

John, Kenda, Ethan, Colby, Linda, Keith

Chapter Nine

Thoughts and Comments

I have tried to remember as much as possible, and while I have talked about a lot of the day-to-day struggles for both the patient and the caregiver, I have tried to maintain Linda's dignity. There are many aspects of the lung transplant world that are difficult to explain and I'm not sure anyone that hasn't lived the experience would ever understand what it's all about. I never really considered the caregiver's role before. It is another life that I think only they understand. I would have never considered myself as a candidate for caregiver, but it turns out God can use anyone for anything. I know now how Moses felt.

The side effects of all the drugs can be very difficult to deal with for both the patient as well as the caregiver. The upset stomach and all the things that go with that can be daily. Some anti-fungal medications cause loss of appetite and just over all "not feel good times." Medications to increase the output of red blood cells cause flu-like symptoms that can last for thirty-six hours. Anti- rejection drugs cause all sorts of problems, Linda's biggest was loss of taste and shaking hands. This made it difficult to perform sewing and other craft activities that caused another source

Thoughts And Comments

of depression. Prednisone causes puffy face, weight gain, and reduced vision. Psychologically these could have been the biggest issues Linda had to deal with. Reading, which had been one of her favorite pastimes was difficult and not worth the effort. Because the doses jumped around so much, it wasn't feasible to have eyeglass prescriptions corrected after each dosage change.

In my case, there were no children still at home or others to manage. The daily household chores had been mine for some time but the desire to do them would wane with each battle that made Linda sick. It seemed that when the patient doesn't feel good, the caregiver experiences sympathy pains. I can't speak for women caregivers, but I know for me I really felt that I was being derelict in my duties as protector and provider. There were so many times that it didn't make any difference what I did; it didn't help.

The insurance, hospitals, and doctors' offices were really pretty understanding. I received a mailbox full of letters and bills on some days and just shook my head. Linda had a medical administration background and had always dealt with these things. So, I didn't have much of an idea what to do with all of the paperwork. I started filing it in order by dates of service and paid the oldest bills when the phone calls started coming. One problem we had was the insurance carrier changed for my company January 1, 2005. We had several bills that went to our old carrier. Then there were the "in-network" versus "out-of-network" issues that made everything difficult. This was an area that caregivers really need assistance with. I suggest a trusted family member take charge of handling the bills and paperwork.

I don't want to scare anyone so badly that they would not consider a transplant. I can't speak for Linda if she would do it all over again, but as for me I can say I would. Had it not been for the transplants Linda would probably not have lived past June 2003. All the difficulties and trials we had been through had brought us closer together. We spent unimaginable hours in the cab of our truck talking and sharing the experience. We spent hours together in waiting rooms and stays in hospitals and clinics that forced us to deal with it together. I would like to have spent the time together doing other things, but we didn't get a choice. So, like I said early on, "I'll take her any way I can get her." When I saw her and our new grandbaby, Ethan, laughing together and just enjoying each other, all the bad memories fade into a dim past that made it all worthwhile.

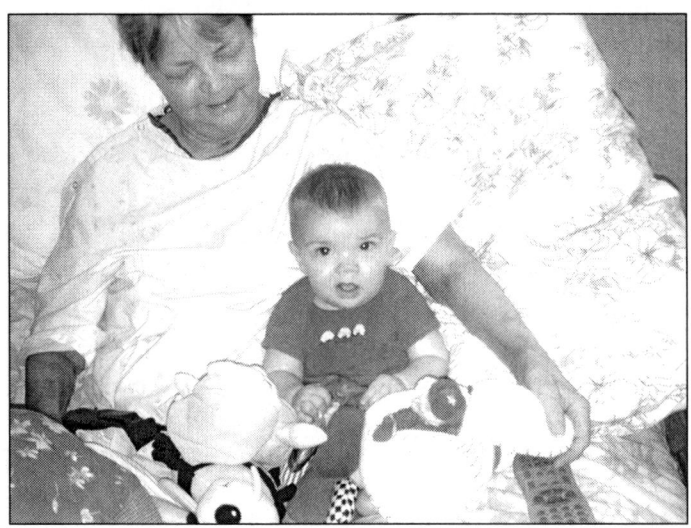

Linda and Ethan

Thoughts And Comments

Linda, Ethan and the bug book

Linda and Ethan feeding the ducks

There are those who would say a transplant is just trading one disease for another. I know that for me it was trading a separating death for a little more life together. There can be an argument made for the quality of life, and no doubt the quality of life for Linda was not quality. But there are times that the quality is as good as it ever was and I will take those memories after June 2003 as a big benefit in my life.

I guess it all came together for me when Linda was her sickest in early 2005. She lay in ICU hooked up to life support for two weeks. I prayed to God that His will would be done. I would give up everything, and I didn't care if we ran through all the insurance money and then everything we had. I could be homeless and on the street if I could just have some more time with her. Then immediately the thought came, "You would trade everything you have for how much time? One year, one month, one week or even one minute?" It was then that I realized I would trade it all for one minute. One minute to tell her how much I loved her, one minute to tell her how much she changed my life, one minute to try and tell her she was my world and my life.

God was gracious and granted us more time. I didn't know how much time we would get, but I knew I would enjoy each and every day as if it was our last. I told her I loved her more than ever before and would take whatever struggles and difficulties we would have from here on out as a true blessing from God. God told me early on before the first transplant when I prayed, "God I can't live without her." His reply was that, "I could live without her, but not without Him." There were no truer words.

Last advice to caregivers is don't get lulled into apathy by the good times. It seems when everything starts going good, I tend to forget how short the good times can be. It's amazing how fast transplant patients can slide down the scale. All can be good in the morning; then, by that evening, you are struggling trying to figure out what to do next. Early on Dr. Angel told me we could wake up one night and have to call 911. Well, it took almost two years before I had to do

Thoughts And Comments

that but, it did happen. From Friday morning to Saturday night everything went from all is well to the scary situation of her not being able to breathe. I guess my point is enjoy the times when all is well and don't take them for granted. Just remember a small change in weather, an unknown reaction to some medication, or nothing at all could send your patient to the hospital for the last time. Those moments you spent together could be your last together on this earth.

I continued to send e-mail updates to friends and family. On November 14, 2005, I informed them that I wished I had better news, but it was what it was. Linda actually had about ten good days in late September and early October where she drove herself to physical therapy twice. She had been getting therapy at Spohn twice a week, but there started to be too much pain in her hips to continue. She had some bleeding in the optic nerves of her eyes, and the doctors immediately discontinued the blood thinner. After further evaluation by an ophthalmologist she was cleared to return to the thinner and spent ten days in the hospital while they obtained the correct level. We went to our regular clinic visit on the fourteenth of October, and the blood test uncovered some high acid and creatin levels that indicated the kidneys were not working properly. When they realized the potassium was too high, they immediately put her in the hospital. Her EKG indicated irregular heartbeats, and that's when we learned that potassium was what was used for the fatal injection for death row. She spent three days in San Antonio while they brought her levels back into range. The hip pain continued, and she also had pain moving around her body from one area to another. They took x-rays in San Antonio that were not conclusive. So, we had an MRI in Corpus Christi on November 2nd that indicated evidence of avascualr necrosis in the femoral heads bilaterally with subchondral serpiginous low signal intensity lines. The involvement on both sides was approximately 75 to 100 percent. The findings seemed to indicate FICAT stage

3 of the avascular necrosis. In a nutshell, she had lost the blood supply to her hip joints and the bone had died. This was not uncommon for patients on high and long doses of anti-rejection drugs and steroids.

The doctors in San Antonio were trying to get Linda an appointment with an orthopedic surgeon that was supposed to be the best in Texas. The first problem was he was booked until February. Dr. Angel pulled strings and said we could get in to see him in a couple or three weeks. It would be an evaluation for a double hip replacement. I wasn't sure Linda would be a good candidate for hip replacement, but she was optimistic, and I wasn't about to rain on that parade. She was pretty down Friday when we received the official word of her condition, but we spent the weekend in Killeen for Ethan's first birthday party. I think he was better medicine for her than anything else.

Linda's resilience never ceased to amaze me. She was already getting things ready for an extended hospital stay and a long recovery time. She had me rearranging furniture and making ready for the next hurdle we had in front of us. She had been buying new clothes and jewelry from TV that always made her feel better. I thanked Mary and Jim for the chocolate, which also always helped. Darcy, my boss at the time, came by and had lunch one day, and that was very nice.

There were still lots of questions that needed answers, although it was ironic that the lungs were doing well and the x-rays continued to look very good. There was a slight decrease in the PFTs, but that was probably due to reduced activity and more pain killers. Linda was on a more regimented dose of pain medication, instead of as needed. It was needed most of the time now. The roller coaster ride continued, and as always, the prayers were appreciated.

By November 23, 2005, Linda was back in the hospital in San Antonio. Due to shortness of breath and bad swelling in her legs (particularly the right leg), we checked in Thursday night about 7:00 PM. Blood draws, X-rays, and ultra sound testing started and continued most of the night. It seemed a sonogram finally revealed a blood clot in her right leg. She had a screen that was supposed to catch these clots and did catch the bigger ones, but the small pieces could get by and proceed to the lung.

She had a pulmonary embolism, and when you only have one and about an eighth of a lung working, it doesn't take much to cause breathing problems. She was already therapeutic with blood thinner, so there wasn't much we could do with that. Cultures were started but didn't indicate an infection until late Saturday. Once again, she was in isolation for VRE, which is one of the nasty resident infections which she battled all the time. IV antibiotics and breathing treatments every six hours were working to get this one under control again. The problem was there was one that could not be identified as to where or what it was. Since these infections continually mutate to battle the medications, this was not unusual. They drew blood from her and tagged it with a radioactive ID. They then injected the blood back into her body. Twenty-four hours later (about 3:30 PM), they took a full-body x-ray and found where the blood collected. The reinjected blood would attach itself to the infection, and the area would be identified. At that point, we were not hopeful to be home by Thanksgiving. Since they would not give her a PIC line for fear of more infections, she would need to continue IVs in the hospital. I couldn't administer the meds at home. We could have had a home health nurse come out, but the isolation issue still needed to be considered. Some good news was that since the blood clot and other infections had cleared, she had not had the pain in her hips, shoulders, elbows, and just about every other joint in her body. The PA for the orthopedic surgeon came by Monday and evaluated her for hip replacement surgery. It seemed she was at a level 3 degeneration of a level 4 scale. They would set her up for home therapy and hopefully do some therapy before the surgery. According to Dr. Angel she could handle the surgery if she recovered to the physical status she had two weeks earlier.

Needless to say, Linda was a little discouraged about spending another holiday in the hospital. It might not have been so bad, but Ethan and his parents would be in town, and they couldn't visit her in isolation. I was not trying to bring everybody down for their Thanksgiving, and we were determined not to be down for ours either. We had so much to be thankful for, and I was reminded that Sunday night at our church Thanksgiving dinner. I could probably write a book about all the things we had to be thankful for, but most of all I'm thankful we have a loving God who knows our hearts' desires and wants to give them to us. I hoped each one of our friends and their families had a Happy Thanksgiving because Linda, our family, and I would.

May 13, 2006 was a very special day. Linda, her mom, and I watched Colby walk across the stage at the American Bank Center when he received his college diploma. He received a Bachelor of Science degree from Texas A&M University in Corpus Christi. He had finally made it, and it wasn't an easy task. Colby showed a lot of determination and some of his "stick-to-itiveness" by completing his college courses and receiving his diploma. There was no one more proud than Linda. It wasn't a good day physically (not many were), but she was so high that day that she pushed through much fatigue and pain to be at that place and time. No one else would ever know. She was beaming and had a great time being there to celebrate the occasion. This was another goal she had accomplished.

Thoughts And Comments

Linda and Colby – Graduation Day!

Chapter Ten

Here We Go Again!

I could look back at the EOB, explanation of benefits, and get exact dates for hospital stays that year, but I don't see that it's critical to the story. Suffice to say, they hadn't been as numerous as the previous year, 2005. I made forty-three trips to San Antonio, and they weren't as long. We did spend Memorial Day weekend in Spohn Hospital in Corpus Christi, which became quite a joke. Everyone told us it was the "in" thing to be in a hospital for the holidays. We also spent Easter in the hospital.

The most repeated sequence of numbers I had said in the past three years seemed to be 12–1–51, Linda's birthday. Sometimes when I was asked for my birth date, I started out with 12–1 and then caught myself. Now, it's 6–15–06 and never before has the sequence of numbers 12–1–51 had such an impact on my life. Linda once again lay in ICU, hooked up to a machine to breathe for her. I turned to the keys of my computer for relief. It was my first entry in 2006, and it seemed that, along with everything else, my writing had gone to the side as a burnout. I had wanted to document

Here We Go Again!

events and keep the journal current, but my fingers wouldn't type the thoughts I had on my mind.

I was at the empty house with nothing to do. Just three days before Linda was home and my time was booked solid. She had become more of an invalid and required much more attention. Although she continued to act like nothing was wrong, I had to help her stand and sit down. She could muster the first stand out of bed each day and always insisted on doing that. I would offer to help, but she would say, "No, I can still do it." I checked my e-mail that night and found scriptures from Kenda. Somehow she knew I was struggling. I knew that God told her to send them to me. That encouraged me to get out the keyboard.

Due to terrible fatigue, I wasn't able to get much down. I had been sitting around the hospital and with the extra stress of trying to get Linda off of the machine that was breathing for her, I was wiped out by the time I got home. I wanted to get started because I owed it to Linda and those who needed inspiration.

June 6, 2006, was another failed attempt to get Linda off the machine. They started weaning her by reducing the amount of sedative she was on about four hours ahead of reducing the load the machine carried. Normally, the machine breathed twelve times a minute for her and when she over-breathed the machine provided added pressure to help her out. The goal was to get her to two breaths by the machine and then if the blood gases were still good, we could pull the tube and disconnect the machine. The first day attempt, she made it to four and the gases were bad. Since you can only make one attempt a day, we tried again the next day. Actually, I guess you could try as many times as you wanted, but the idea to sedate her was to let the body rest to hopefully rebuild so the next attempt would be successful. The second day she made it to two, but the gases-were still bad. The ABG was a test to measure the amount of CO_2 in the blood, and it was drawn from an artery. The lungs had to bring in oxygen and take out gas as well. Since it is so deep, it was not a pleasant draw at all. Linda's veins and arteries had both given out. The first attempt, they drew blood gas every thirty minutes. The next day, we made it to ten and the gases were already bad, so everything was put on hold for the weekend.

Monday morning was a good one, and Linda was able to communicate some. I had to ask yes and no questions and she nodded her head. Sometimes, I could get her to open her eyes. I took a CD player down to her room and brought some of her favorite music. The nurse said her heart rate dropped ten beats per minute when the music was on. Her eyesight had been bad for quite some time, and I had been reading some books at bedtime. I purchased *The Man Called Cash* (after I rented *Walk the Line*) and two books by Max Lucado, God's Power and *Grace for the Moment.* Max's books are daily inspirationals and these daily insights from Max lifted my spirits and encouraged me anew each day. I highly recommend these two or another Christian writer to offer a different perspective on your daily vision based on scripture that speaks to the heart.

James 5:16

When a believing person prays, great things happen.

How often do people run to God as a last resort? We should go to him first and things that are greater than we can imagine will happen.

Matthew 21:22

And all things, whatsoever ye shall ask in prayer, believing, ye shall receive.

This is not a blank check to ask for anything you want and expect to get it. When we believe deeply in God and his power our prayers are more in line with his will. His will is to give us what's best for us and him. I don't know how many times I've seen people pray for healing and I have had to wonder if healing is in God's will?

As I opened *Grace for the Moment* the page fell open to January 16th, "God's Good Timing."

Luke 18:7

And shall not God avenge his elect, that cry to him day and night, and yet he is longsuffering over them?

We can know God hears our prayers when we are truly his children that have confessed our sins and sought forgiveness. He will do what is best regardless if we see or hear anything taking place.

Finally I would like to share the June 16th scripture.

Romans 3:23–24

for all have sinned, and fall short of the glory of God;[24] being justified freely by his grace through the redemption that is in Christ Jesus:

We often want to grade sin. It's easy to see other sins that I might not commit (murder, adultery, or theft) as worse than the "little" sins I commit. Truth is all sin separates us from God and "all" have sinned which prevents us from knowing him intimately. Hallelujah verse twenty four declares we are justified (just as if I've never sinned) and by his grace (nothing I can do) I have redemption. What peace this truth brings to me. Regardless of what happens I have a relationship with God the creator who loves me and desires the best for us.

Once again I would like to thank everyone for their prayers and support. We know God's perfect will is what we want and will receive. Someday I hope I can share with you how merciful God has been. I would also like to thank Kenda for all her spiritual support.

Kenda replied to an email that she really liked the devotionals I had shared. She said she prayed God would be glorified in all this! She said, "Can you imagine if people get saved (especially in our family) as a result of all this hardship?"

Kenda helped me get back where I belonged. I was struggling to find what I needed, and her scriptures and songs woke me up. It was amazing how muddled my thinking had become.

Micah 6:8

He hath showed thee, O man, what is good; and what doth Jehovah require of thee, but to do justly, and to love kindness, and to walk humbly with thy God?

I sat in Linda's room most of the day, just being with her. I started reliving the week and jotted some things down. Going back to Monday night June 12, 2006, at 8:45 PM.

June 12, 2006, was a Monday I will never forget. It began a twenty-five day experience that brought miracles and answered prayers beyond what I or anyone else could imagine. This is a testimony of the events and miracles that confirm God was in control. Regardless of what we think we know, we are specks in a universe that He created. As such, we have only Him to thank for every breath we take.

The problem with transplant patients is they end up taking poison to stay alive. The very organs that had been

Here We Go Again!

placed in their bodies are constantly trying to be rejected by the host body they are designed to save. It is a strange relationship that has both physical and mental complications. Medicines have been developed that suppress the body's immune system to prevent the organ from being rejected. Rejection is simply the body attacking the foreign object, believing it is dangerous to the survival of the host. This is how we defend ourselves against infection and diseases. Unfortunately, most medications we take into our bodies have side effects.

Many of the medications are damaging to our liver and kidneys because of the extra load placed on these two organs. Other side effects include blood clotting, which can be very serious. If a clot forms and breaks loose from the wall of an artery or vein, it can travel through the body to the heart or lungs and sometimes the brain. In simple terms, this stops the blood flow, and everyone knows stopped blood flow is not a good thing. The only way to prevent blood clots is to thin the blood. If the blood is kept thin enough, theoretically it cannot clot. The drug most often used to thin blood is called Coumadin. It is basically the same drug used in rat poison. I don't know if you understand how rat poison works, but it basically thins the blood to where it will not support life. The rat usually starts to hemorrhage inside and bleeds to death.

Of course, the dosage in humans is closely monitored, and most of the time hemorrhaging is avoided. As I stated earlier, Linda's liver and kidneys were both marginal and trying to regulate the Coumadin was almost impossible. The desired number was 10 (not critical to this story what that represents other than a target number), and she had to have blood drawn to find out what that number was. The numbers were all over the place. Linda could take 1 mg. of Coumadin and the number would be subtherapeutic (under 5) and then she could take 2 mg. and the number would go through the roof (100—very dangerous). We would be at the blood draw

Fair Weather Ahead

clinic every morning at 6:30 waiting on them to open. That wasn't an easy task in itself, but that's another story. Monday morning the blood had been drawn, and we waited for the results. Since the normal turn around for test results was four days, we always ordered the results stat. That allowed us to see the results the same day. Around 3:00 PM the call came that the number was over 100. That meant we could not administer any Coumadin that day and we would retest the next day. The liver was the suspect for causing these swings. That was not unusual, and there was no sense of alarm; it was just life as we knew it. Dr. Geneser would tell everyone, "Welcome to Linda's world!"

Linda had been in bed about an hour, and we were kicked back watching TV. She called out for me to come into her room. She had coughed up a piece of something that was best described as a membrane. It wasn't mucus, but it was about 2 inches long and 1/8 inch wide. We studied it for quite a while and then decided we didn't know what it was. I did, however, think it was from her lungs, and that caused me great concern. I returned to the den and about ten minutes later she called me back. Her nose was bleeding, and I looked down her throat. It was coated in blood, and I'm still thinking it's all coming from the lungs. We finally figured out the source of the blood was from her nose. After thirty minutes, we hadn't managed to slow it down.

I called Dr. Geneser and told him what was going on. He said if things got worse, take her to the ER. This was always one of the biggest decisions we had to make. We spent so much time in the hospital, and neither one of us ever wanted to go. We also had talked about one day the trip to the hospital would be the last one. So, we believed if we didn't ever go it wouldn't be the last trip. The bleeding was minimal, but we never could get it to totally stop. About 10:30 I decided we had to go. I knew I would not be able to sleep wondering if she would start bleeding and bleed out without even waking

Here We Go Again!

up. We loaded up and headed to the hospital. On the way, I called our doctors on call.

We arrived at the emergency room about 11:00 PM, and much to our delight, we were met by our doctor. Nothing against ER doctors, but it is such a comfort to see your regular doctor there in time of need. The bleeding had been continuous, and although it wasn't a large flow, it had made quite a mess by now. We had switched to wash clothes and now to towels. There was a lot of blood. The first order was to give her three to four units of frozen plasma. This would be the fastest way to thicken the blood. A nurse was assigned to holding Linda's nose. Other nurses and our doctor were busy taking blood pressure, drawing blood, and inserting an IV. It was always such a relief for me when I could hand her care off to the doctors and nurses. This was a handoff that occurred often, and it was always a load off of my shoulders. Having someone's life in your hands is the most stressful experience you can have in life. Linda's life was in my hands daily. Even though I didn't want to go there, anytime I could have her cared for in the hospital was a tremendous lift. It was another one of those roller coasters that we continually rode.

The bleeding was stopped in about thirty minutes, and everything calmed down to a dull roar. Seriously, there was a lot less tension in the air once the bleeding was under control. You never know when someone's blood is so thin that a bleed will not be able to be stopped. Our doctor said he wanted to keep Linda at least overnight. I thought it was a little strange when he said he wanted to keep her in ICU. I asked him about it, and he said they would monitor her closer in ICU. I felt better.

We made it to ICU a little after midnight. Linda slept with an oxygen mask with about four units of O_2. I answered all the questions again and realized I knew Linda's medical history better than my own. It always amazed the nurses how well I could provide answers to their questions. Their whole demeanor changed when they realized I was more than a casual spouse. We completed all the forms there in the room, and I woke Linda up about 1:30 AM to tell her I was going to take a nap. She said that was good, and we kissed, and said I love you to each other. I was first (inside joke). I made it home about 1:30 AM or so and finally got to bed about 2:00.

Dr. Geneser, Linda, and I had lengthy discussions during our Memorial Day stay at the hospital. This wasn't our first discussion with him about what Linda wanted done when the time came. She felt the chance in San Antonio last year saved her life, and she wanted another chance. So Dr. Geneser said that he would do everything he could to save her. He then said after Linda became unable to communicate, I would be called on to make the tough decisions and wanted to know if I could do that. I said yes I could because I felt I knew Linda best and would carry out her wishes. I don't think I fully understood what I had agreed to do.

My phone rang at 5:45 AM. The nurse on the other end said I should come to the hospital. Linda was having some difficulty. I jumped up and was at the hospital within twenty minutes. The monitors had shown that Linda had stopped breathing and had momentarily slipped into a coma. The nurse that arrived at her bedside first said her eyes were dilated and fixed, which was an indication that she was dead. They immediately revived her and she did come back. Our doctor ordered her to have an emergency MRI run on her brain. He suspected an aneurism since her blood was so thin. This is a rupture of a blood vessel in the brain and would result in loss of blood to the brain. The MRI did not indicate an aneurism. Since she was unable to breathe on her own, they returned her to ICU and had to intubate her. This wasn't the first time Linda had been intubated. She was in a coma in San Antonio in 2005 for ten days. She fought being intubated every time, and this was no different. She kept telling

Here We Go Again!

me she would be all right and not to let them do it. It was a terrible situation to be in. She so wanted to not do it, but the doctors and nurses knew she couldn't live without it. I had to authorize them to do it.

I struggled with those last minutes of communication about the intubation for three days, and then I figured it out. She did the same thing in San Antonio a little over a year ago. When Dr. Angel said we were going to intubate her she argued she didn't need it. She said she was breathing fine now and didn't need it. Dr. Angel said he would give her twenty minutes to get her gases down, and then he would intubate. He came back in ten minutes and said we would have to do it. I will never forget her saying, "I don't want to be intubated," and looking at me for help. I looked at her with huge tears in my eyes and said, "I don't want to either, but we have to." This current request for the mask was her saying, "I don't need to be intubated; I just need an oxygen mask." Since that morning, I have put a lot of things together and unfortunately she did need to be intubated, and she didn't realize it at the time. Dr. Geneser told me later if she had been at home she wouldn't have lasted long enough for the ambulance to get to the house. There was a nurse in the room talking to her that morning. Linda had made a comment, and they were laughing, and the mood was light. I'm sure Linda thought she would be coming home that day. The nurse said she turned around and Linda was in respiratory failure and her eyes had already dilated and fixed. It happened that fast. She grabbed the machine, and she was intubated that fast. It saved her life, for the moment.

It was only Tuesday morning, and little did I know what lay in store for us. One of the problems with intubating someone was getting them off of the breathing machine. Intubation is the attaching of a breathing machine that breathes for a person. If the person cannot get enough oxygen, for whatever reason, the machine can be adjusted to provide the oxygen. Oxygen can be regulated and administered directly to the lungs. The number of breaths per minute can also be regulated and thus keep the patient alive. The problem is the body might not be capable of supporting itself and sometimes becomes reliant on the machine to do the work, especially if the body is fatigued or damaged, as in Linda's case. Our doctor said we would let Linda rest for the day and try to remove the machine the next day. He said it was important that she had all the strength she could muster before we tried to remove the support.

The plan was to get the machine down to providing four breaths per minute. Obviously, Linda's body would be breathing more, but the rest of the breathing would be on her to provide. Once the machine was down to four breaths per minute, we would check her oxygen levels. What surprised me was that I couldn't remember what number we were looking for. The minimum saturation we could have was an 80. This would be on a small amount of oxygen, and that would tell us she could support herself if the machine was not helping. The blood draw had to come from an artery instead of a vein. This is the blood supply leaving the heart that would have the most oxygen in it. Knowing what the minimum was to support the body, we would know if she was there or not. The problem was the artery in the arm was deep and not easy to hit, and it was painful. Although, Linda was in an induced coma she would still grimace, and you could tell it hurt. Wednesday, we did manage to get the machine down to four breaths per minute but the oxygen level wasn't satisfactory.

Thursday was worse; we couldn't even get the machine down to twelve breaths per minute and maintain the oxygen levels needed. Each day after an attempt, it was just rest for Linda and praying that she would regain enough strength for the next day's attempt. Friday morning came with much anticipation. It was even worse! We could not reduce the

Here We Go Again!

number of breaths by the machine lower than eighteen without the oxygen levels falling. We would always take a sample before we started and then a couple of times as the machine support was reduced. The initial results were not good. So that was it for the day.

Our doctor advised us to let Linda rest all weekend, and we would try again Monday. Maybe she would build up enough strength to breathe on her own. I have not mentioned a lot of the emotions and stress that week had brought on me. I think anyone who can understand what has been going on here can realize what we all must have been going through. Lack of sleep, lack of appetite, and really lack of interest in anything else was my life. I picked up the paper one day in the waiting room, and just stared at it. I tried to read it, but the words on the paper didn't even make sense. I was in another world.

I told everyone to just stay home over the weekend. There were lots of friends and family always supporting me, but this was going to be a quiet weekend. I encouraged them to have as normal a weekend as possible and spend it with their families. I wanted this weekend for just Linda and me. I talked to Linda a lot when she was in comas. I have heard that people in comas can sometimes hear when talking to them. Although it wasn't much, I would just tell her something that I had done that day and about the kids. I would tell her who was out in the waiting room and who had been by to see her. I found out later she didn't hear a thing, but I guess it was good for me. I read to her from a book we had been reading together. It was the story of Johnny Cash, *I Walk the Line*. I also read scriptures and I would pray with her. I spent most of Saturday and Sunday just sitting next to her holding her hand and talking, sometimes not talking at all.

On Sunday, June 18th, I just wanted to sit with her and hold her hand and spend time alone. I walked down to the solarium at the end of the hall. I watched kids in the park

Fair Weather Ahead

playing and cars driving by. I watched people sailing and fishing while others jogged and carried on like nothing was the matter. I thought, *What's wrong with all of you? Don't you know my soul mate, my sweetheart, the love of my life is lying up here dying? How can you just act like nothing is wrong?* Then the words started to come to me, and I wrote this poem to try to express my thoughts. That was when I sat down and penned, "When Will You and I Get Fair Weather." Someone asked me once how long it took to pen this poem. My first answer was about fifteen minutes, but that wasn't accurate. It actually took thirty six years. It flowed to the paper naturally, but the fact is my emotions were very raw, and all the years of love poured out. It was straight from the heart, and Linda loved it.

When Will You and I Get Fair Weather?

The waves don't stop rolling and the trees don't stop growing,
Just because one person no longer breathes.
The world doesn't notice when just a single life comes in, or leaves.

The children continue to play and the old folks will always pray,
The rest of the world says, "It's just another day."

Just another day you can choose to throw away
You are only given so much time and time is how we pay.

Time is one account we can't balance to know,
When we arrive no one says "here's your bank, spend it till you go."

Here We Go Again!

Tomorrow has no guarantee; the only thing for sure is it's not free,

People budget silly paper and coins, careful how to spend.
Yet they throw time away, like it's never going to end.

Where did you spend your time today?
Did you spend it wisely or did you throw it away?

Did you say I love you more than once, for no reason at all?
Did you say, "You're beautiful just the way you are,"
Did you make time for one phone call?

The things of love are not of this world, they just can't understand.
How does compassion, love and care make sense to any man.

It can't make sense without the love of Christ,
He is the one that is the light.

Oh how I fail when I spend my time on things other than love,
Oh how I fail when I operate in this world instead of with guidance from above.

The waves don't stop rolling and the trees don't stop growing,

But the angels in heaven rejoice because another souls taken their leave,
They leave the pain and suffering of this old world and really start to breathe,

God notices when a single sparrow falls, so he waits for us as he gently calls.
Now we know our bank is full and we have unlimited time to spend together,
We are again as one and eternity is ours, with nothing but fair weather.

Linda I can't wait to see you again.

I signed it with that last sentence, because at the time I wasn't sure if I would see her again this side of heaven.

Monday morning, June 19, 2006, started out badly. Since our last attempt on Friday, the "Machine" had been on twelve breaths per minute and all was well. Friday morning, the machine was at 16 and the oxygen was at forty percent, up from thirty-five percent. I had learned what to watch for on all the monitors and could tell things were not good. Colby arrived at 6:00 AM on Sunday, and had quite a story about his trip. Short version is bad weather had Houston Intercontinental closed so they had to land in Layfette, Louisiana. After his plane sat on the tarmac for three hours, his connection to Corpus Christi was cancelled. The next flight they had him on was Monday. He caught the city bus to downtown Houston at midnight and from there rode the Greyhound to Corpus Christi.

Linda's blood gases were climbing and more support was needed just to keep them in a safe range. There was no attempt at removing the ventilator that day, and it was obvious that unless something changed, she would be relying totally on the machine. Kenda, who was eight and a half months pregnant, met with her OB early Monday morning

Here We Go Again!

and would meet Kate, her cousin, in Austin to ride down that afternoon. They arrived about 3:00 PM.

On Tuesday, June 20, 2006, there was no change, and I knew Dr. Geneser would be in about 9:00 AM to discuss our path forward. Kenda, Colby, and I talked the night before and were in agreement that if things were not better today, then we had to remove the machine. Although, the final word still had to come from me, I felt it was important that we all agree. The conversation began in the hall outside Linda's room with Dr. Geneser, Kenda, Charlotte and me. Dr. Geneser went back to Linda's first visit in his office. He spent a lot of time explaining how we arrived to this point. I admired him so much for his ability to forget the rest of the world and act as though we were all that mattered. He was constantly doing that and gave an enormous amount of time to our family and me. Before he was through, Charla, Sharon, and Mark had joined in the conversation.

After about twenty minutes of explanation he looked at me and asked, "What do you want to do?" I said, "I know Linda would not want to live like this and in fact would be asking why the delay. Why haven't you already done something?" I told him to remove the support. He agreed, and Mark said, "As much as you felt that you had made a decision, you really didn't have a choice." I thought it helped at first, but then it really didn't.

I asked everyone to go say goodbye as I wanted to be the only one with her when she passed away. All the family and friends spent time with her and left the hospital per my request. It was about 3:00 PM when they removed the support, and I sat by her bed with her hand in mine. I somehow expected her to be gone in an hour or two. The nurses made their shift change, and she was still here. I asked the night nurse about the time, and he said he had seen it take two minutes, but sometimes it could take two days. I hadn't been told that.

I can't even tell you what Tuesday night and Wednesday morning were like. I didn't sleep, but I didn't want to. I thought for sure Linda would be gone any minute, and it just kept dragging on. I would struggle with the limited visiting hours of ICU. I had to leave at 9:00 PM, and could not get into to see Linda till 8:30 AM. I would show up about 6:30 AM to go in and spend a few minutes with her, hold her hand, and tell her good morning. I was usually gone in five minutes and would wait in the waiting room until the official time. One morning, a nurse approached and informed me I would have to leave because it wasn't visiting hours. I didn't handle that very well and later had to apologize.

The days kept dragging on. There were always some friends and family members in the waiting room. We were all just sitting around waiting for the final word, and the word never came. I was chastised several times because I wouldn't eat. Imagine that, me not hungry. Mark even threatened once to tell Kenda if I didn't eat breakfast. It is amazing how time doesn't matter, I didn't know if it was day or night and I didn't care. I tried to read a newspaper that was in the waiting room, and nothing made sense when I tried to comprehend the words. It was like my attention span wasn't long enough for the letters to be recognized to form words in my head. I was in limbo, and nothing mattered.

Somewhere along the way, I had a routine established. I would wake up at 4:00 AM every morning without an alarm or anything. I would just sit up in bed and be wide awake. I would get dressed and head to the hospital. Since I couldn't stay in Linda's room very long, most of the time was spent in the waiting room or roaming the halls. I couldn't stay away, but when I got there, I couldn't stay put. Since I expected something to happen any minute of the day or night, it was torture.

Here We Go Again!

On Friday night, June 23, 2006, they moved Linda out of ICU and we went to the telemetry floor. Since we knew all the staff on the floor, it was like coming home again. It brought comfort to know that she would be around familiar people when she finally did pass away.

Linda had been off of any medications or breathing support since 3:00 PM Tuesday, and the madness continued. Her arms were swelling and were very large. I had seen them bigger when she was in San Antonio last year. I didn't think the skin could stretch so much. We were just trying to keep her comfortable with morphine and fluids through an IV. Nothing seemed to ever change. Family and friends were hanging around talking about many different topics and except for the daily visit by the doctor, no real meaningful information surfaced. I knew we couldn't just sit there and look at each other. Friday afternoon, Linda's arm swelled so much it pushed the IV out of her arm. There was some discussion about trying to reestablish it, but after conversation with Colby and Kenda we decided not to. Since we had agreed Linda had received her last stick Tuesday, it didn't seem necessary.

Now Linda was totally independent of any support or medications except for an oxygen mask with forty percent oxygen. I decided it was time to say farewell.

Farewell to Linda
No, see ya later is more like it.

What a great life we have had together. You raised me while I raised you. How blind was I when we started this journey together? I was blinded by your physical beauty and had no idea of your inner beauty and really didn't care at that time. Young men hardly ever look very deep and I was guilty of that. What a marvelous 36 years it's been. You taught me

Fair Weather Ahead

gentleness, kindness, faithfulness, and nurturing. You gave me the two biggest blessing of my life.

I don't know how one person can have such an effect on another person as you did on me. Anything I have become, anything I have achieved, anything I have is greatly due to you.

Your unselfishness, generosity, and never-ending giving to others were only exceeded by your desire to be a wife, mother and grandmother, and oh what a wife, mother, and grandmother you are. You have inspired me, encouraged me, supported me, and taught me what real courage is. You have passed these characteristics on to our children, and they will pass them on to theirs. What a legacy you leave behind!

You could look any challenge straight in the eye and never back down. You followed me wherever I led you and loved every minute of it because you believed in me, which gave me strength and courage for the day. You loved your family above yourself and would have given up your life for them without hesitation.

Your engineering mind and relentless desire for the details made you a perfectionist by choice and calling, which provided much joy for you. I have never known anyone with such a unique blend of romanticism and realism. My biggest regret is it took me so long to understand and enjoy the romantic side. I feel like I cheated both of us.

As for our life together, I have only one regret and that is we only had 36 years together instead of 63 years, but I trust God knows what's best for us both. You touched so many lives and will continue to influence many of us. Unfortunately, your huge will to live wasn't matched by your body's ability to continue living here in this world. Now, you have moved on to a place with no pain and are receiving the gifts you so deserve. Now, you have new lungs that won't be rejected and no medications required.

Here We Go Again!

I know beyond a shadow of a doubt that we will be together again and will look forward to our reunion every day. Our Heavenly Father said, "I go to prepare a place for you." He just received the best help he ever had.

It's not Farewell, Adios or even good bye; it's See Ya Later.

I Love You, Keith

The stress became unbearable at times. I would break out in a sweat mostly on my back and head. I found myself clinching my teeth, and I wasn't even aware of it. Nausea was common, and my heart fluttering was always there if I thought about it. One night I penned these words during a darker hour.

Love That Exceeds Understanding

I have struggled to find another way of communicating my sorrow, pain and loneliness that exceeds man's feeble attempt to express.

The emotions run together in a twisting, squirming roller coaster that spirals out of control into the deepest part of my soul.

They wrestle in an unending battle for my attention through my consciousness and just when it seems one is on top and can have power over the others they all tumble out of control.

Crashing in the pit of my stomach they rise and fall over and over again until my wits are challenged just to breath. Sometimes reasoning is unattainable and the simplest task seems impossible.

Fair Weather Ahead

The fluttering wings of the emotions can be felt in my heart and the darkness can't cover the ugliness residing inside.
What possible purpose does this never ending torture have?
What possible profit is all of this? Why the maddening life?

Wait! What is that, a flicker of light? I can't make it out but it beckons.
I approach with caution for fatigue has clouded my judgment.
What if it's more pain, sorrow and loneliness disguised as hope?

I can feel the warmth now as the flicker has grown into a blaze.
Still not sure what it means or how it will influence me.
Then before I can completely comprehend, it engulfs my spirit.

The darkness is blasted out by the brilliant light of the hugest bon fire bright as the sun over the earth. The heat singes the wings of despair and all its attendants and they fall to the bottomless pit with no power over me.

Appreciation, gratitude, humbleness and peace are abundantly multiplied by Love.
I sit back and drink in the new found peace and realize I am blessed by a merciful God that loves me and has always wanted and always will want the best for me.
I had allowed all those terrible ugly emotions to spring up from a willingness to enjoy pity. Who am I to allow pity when God paid such a price?

Here We Go Again!

How did such a miracle of relief find me when I was so lost to reason? Where and what was that flicker of light, I ask God?
In the simplest purest form of communicating he makes me understand it was a caring person's prayer that He would console me.
Someone unidentified to me had requested to the Creator of the universe that He come and comfort me. Humbly I bow asking forgiveness. How could I forget?

God just says "trust in me," "never let love and faithfulness leave you."
Love that exceeds understanding!

It was Saturday, June 24, 2006, and I couldn't think of anything different to say than yesterday or the day before. Linda just kept on breathing and hanging on. I had been worried about Kenda and Ethni, who still wasn't born, so I convinced Kenda to go home and have a healthy baby. John, Kenda, Ethan, and Ethni went home sometime Saturday morning. Colby was scheduled to fly out Monday, but he was already making sounds about staying longer. I was starting to show signs of wearing out from lack of sleep and tremendous stress had me doing weird stuff. I would go to the truck in the parking garage and before I could get the truck started I would go back into the hospital. I wanted to leave, but couldn't. One time I turned around and went back after I got on the freeway. I would go back and couldn't stay. Linda had been communicating, at least I thought, with head shakes and some conversation. I had talked to Dr. Geneser about it, and he said he wouldn't put much faith in the contact. She could be drifting in and out of death and she was on a regular dose (hourly) of morphine. It would tear me up when I thought she was talking to me. She was so nice and cordial, even in that darkest hour. She would be grimacing as if she was uncomfortable. So, I would adjust her pillow or move her arm and out of the unconsciousness would come a small almost childlike, "Thank you." That would just tear my guts out.

I finally had something that confirmed, for me that it really wasn't Linda's person or personal self I was communicating with. It was our little "I love you" game. Each morning, we would see which one of us could say "I love you" first. Either way the response was always, "I love you, too." Although, sometimes if she beat me to it, I would respond with, "Not as much as I love you." We connected, and she wasn't doing that now. I would say "I love you" and she would respond with that small voice "Thank you." I knew then she didn't recognize me as me. She would have responded with "I love you, too." This brought on more mixed feelings and confusion as to what I felt. It was a blessing that she wasn't conscious enough to know what was going on, but then there I was again touching her and not able to talk to her. Somehow, the day ended, and night time arrived, and I went home. I had started living with my cell phone in my hand, just waiting on it to ring, so they could tell me it was over.

On Sunday, June 25, 2006, I woke up at 4:00 AM, same as always. I'm not sure how much I slept; I could never tell. I tried to get up, and it was like a ton of weight was on my chest. My legs weighed a ton, and I couldn't move them. I felt like I had the flu and a headache that would kill a mule. I had a death grip on my cell phone, but it wouldn't ring. I rolled and tumbled around in bed for a couple of hours and must have drifted off to sleep. I would drift out of consciousness myself and remember praying that God would go ahead and take me so this misery would end. I couldn't take it anymore. Just about the time I had that thought, my phone rang. It was Kenda; she never calls me on Sunday morning. I don't remember what she said, but it seems like she read me some scriptures. It had the same effect, what-

Here We Go Again!

ever she said. About thirty seconds after she hung up, Mark Miller, my pastor, called; he never calls on Sunday morning. Mark prayed with me, and it seemed to lift me up from the deepest, darkest hour of my life. Never in my life had I felt so physically, mentally, and emotionally drained. I could not move, I could not think, and trying to figure out what to do next was impossible. At least now there was some peace. I drifted off to sleep, and Colby woke me up about 10:00 AM. He said we had to do something. I said what are you talking about? He said mom was talking to him last night. I said yes she has been talking some, but it's not her. He said it was her. I dragged myself out of bed and moved to the recliner in the den. He was pacing the floor like a caged animal. He said he went by the hospital about midnight last night, and mom was having a conversation with him. I said I know we have been getting responses, but it's really not her. He was very adamant and insisted that he was conversing with her, and we couldn't just let her die alone in that room. I asked him what she said that made him think it was her. He said he asked her what color her 1969 Chevelle was, and she said, "Silver." I'm sure my jaw dropped. I jumped up, put on some clothes, and away we went.

When we arrived, Linda was sleeping. I was still reluctant to expect anything, but Colby kept insisting that they had an intelligent conversation. We stood out in the hall somewhat arguing over if it was her or not. I didn't want him to get his hopes up for something that I didn't think was possible. After about thirty minutes of waiting, my phone rang, and I was talking when Colby went in to check on her. She was awake. I finished my phone call and walked in to find Linda and Colby sitting there talking about an old black and white movie on the TV. I sat next to the bed and listened as they talked. Linda was telling Colby the actors' names and what movie they were watching. I know my eyes must have been as big as a plate. I was amazed. As I watched and listened I started laughing. Linda turned to Colby and said, "What's he laughing at?"

Linda had overcome the routine morphine dose and had been without medications, nutrition, or life support for four days. She had been without any hydration since Friday afternoon and had miraculously sat up and started talking. I immediately went to the nurse's station and asked them to page the doctor. I asked them to page him three times before he finally called back. It probably wasn't that long, but I was a little impatient then. Dr. Geneser was out of town, and Dr. Wong was covering. He called back, and I told him Linda was awake, and I would like to get some labs drawn and get medications started again. He asked, "Does this mean the no stick order was removed?" I said, " Yes!"

The IV nurse showed up first. She said, "I don't think I can get an IV started with those arms that big." I told her just do your best, and maybe it will work. Then the nurse that draws blood gas came in, and she had the same fears. I don't see any way to get a blood gas sample. With the IV nurse working on her left arm and the blood gas on her right, they went to sticking. The blood gas nurse made several attempts and finally called for help. A young man showed up and hit the artery on the first try. We were all jumping for joy. After he left, the IV nurse moved to the other arm. She was working inside the arm above the elbow. I received a phone call and walked out of the room. When I came back in, she had the IV going. I said, "Oh, thank you so much." She said, "Thank God because I couldn't have done it without praying. There was no way for me to find that vein without Him guiding the needle."

By the end of Sunday, June 25, 2006, the saline drip had been started again and after some time the blood gases came back. They were actually better than last Tuesday when she was on the ventilator. Needless to say, Linda had been lying there since Tuesday with no medications of any kind, no

Here We Go Again!

nutrition, and no saline since Friday night. She was better than when we unplugged the support. We called everyone to come down. I don't know for sure what I was thinking. It might have been that in my mind this could be the final surge of energy I've heard about. I wanted everyone to see her and talk to her even if it was for the last time. We probably overdid it. I called out to Dr. Wong as he walked down the hall leaving, "Thank tou!" He looked over his shoulder and said, "Thank God, not me; I didn't do anything." He had told me earlier there was no medical reason for Linda to be alive.

Monday, June, 26, 2006, through Thursday, Linda constantly improved. Dr. Geneser had returned from his weekend out of town and was very surprised to see Linda was still with us. He said he had no idea she would still be alive, much less in this good of shape. Thursday, Dr. Geneser asked if we wanted to go home. Do what? My shock must have been very obvious because Linda questioned me why I didn't want her to come home. It wasn't that I didn't want her home; it was just hard to think about going home when I thought for so long we would be having a funeral. We went home Friday, June 30, 2006.

Ethni was on the way, and I borrowed a travel trailer from Jim and set it up in Kenda and John's driveway. We arrived Thursday, July 6, 2006, and the medical world thought we were crazy for making that trip. I replied, "I'm not telling a person that just faced the grim reaper and sent him packing that she couldn't go see her new grandbaby." Linda struggled with some things, but really did exceptionally well for just having come back from the dead. Ethni was born Friday, July 7, 2006. We stayed all week! It was great, and since we stayed in the trailer we had lots of quality time in the evenings. Another goal met!

Keith, Linda and Ethni Kate one day old

Chapter Eleven

We Knew This Day Would Come!

On October 29, 2006, things started out normal, as Sunday mornings had been for a while. It was the usual routine with a few exceptions. Linda had been fighting an infection, and we had not yet identified the problem. She was hallucinating mildly, which started on Wednesday. By Friday night, she was really bad. Strangely enough she was seeing people who were still alive. I have since learned that usually people in her condition see deceased loved ones. She never did. Mostly, Colby and I were involved in some type of accident. She woke me up one morning sobbing terribly. I ran into her room to see what the problem was. I was scared to death to see what I would find. When I walked in she said, " Hold my hand." When I grabbed her hand, she said, "Oh, it really is you." She had dreamed that someone had made me drink something in front of her and I fell dead to the floor. From then on I slept on a pallet by her bed, which turned out to be the best thing I could have done.

Linda had been pretty much unable to stand by herself for about nine months. Six months earlier, I would help her stand, and she would walk from the bedroom to the den. The past three months she had been unable to stand or walk. She had struggled with the use of her hands, and this was something worse than not being able to walk. The inability to do her handiwork, sewing and crocheting, was devastating. Due to pain, she had lost the use of her right arm and with limited sight, any handiwork was a major effort. She managed to complete a few projects with much effort and pain. I watched her work for about five minutes and rest for ten. Those last projects were true labors of love that cost her dearly.

The hospital stay was, again, just routine to administer antibiotics and fluids. She improved some from Sunday to Monday, then really leveled out for the rest of the stay. She would stay very still, which was the best way for her to conserve energy. That was something Dr. Angel had talked to her about two years ago, and she had mastered it. She had learned to get by with little, or, sometimes, I think, no air. Her body had also adapted to surviving with high gas levels. We learned that in the June incident. She would keep from panicking when I knew she wanted to so badly. When you need air and you draw with all your strength and nothing is there, that is scary. I remember a tech in San Antonio wanted to experience that feeling as best he could. He took a belt and strapped it around his chest. He pulled it tight and tried to breath. I was amazed at his desire to understand his patient's struggles. That must be pretty accurate because many times Linda talked about a tightness in her chest that would not let her lungs expand. Just think about trying to breathe lying flat on the floor with someone sitting on your chest. Linda had experienced that feeling for so long.

I had them insert a feeding tube Wednesday because she hadn't really eaten since Thursday of the previous week. There were some small meals and snacks, but nothing that would sustain her to help fight an infection. She would at least get nutrition that would give her some strength. There

We Knew This Day Would Come!

was something that made her feel like she was choking when she swallowed. This had been getting worse for about a week, but the X-rays would not confirm a problem. We were crushing her pills and working them through the small tube. Since the tube was so small, it was a very tedious effort. If it became plugged, we would have to replace it, and I don't think we could have convinced Linda to do it again.

The blood draws had become more difficult, and her arms were bruising something terrible from all the attempts. She was asking me to constantly cover them so they would not be seen. The IV needed to be changed, and two different IV nurses had been trying for two days to get a new one started, to no avail. Everyone was wondering what we would do if the other IV blew out. With the amount of antibiotics and fluids we had going into her, it was possible at any time. Due to the risk of infection, Friday would be the must-change date. Friday came and went without a new IV.

There was no real change on Friday. Moving Linda for anything had become an impossible task. She continually refused to be bathed and would not let us reposition her in the bed. If we tried to move her at all, it was as if we were stacking a ton of weight on her chest, and she could not breathe. It was the worst I had ever seen. I really had a feeling this was the time and stayed in the room with her every night. I felt like we didn't have much time left, and I wanted to spend all I could with her. Our activity together had become watching TV. We had our favorite shows and discussed them at great length. We continued doing this even in the hospital. So, I couldn't imagine not watching TV without her.

That afternoon, Dr. Geneser came by and said we were at a crossroads and we had some decisions to make. He said medically there was nothing else we could do (déjà vu). He had suggested a bronchoscopy (bronc) earlier in the week, but Linda and I both refused the procedure. Neither of us felt like the risk was worth the reward of what the bronc could tell us. I seriously doubted she could survive the trauma of a bronc. It was plain to see Dr. Geneser was struggling with what to do next, and I believed he felt like this was it but didn't want to give up. Up to this point, Linda had always been full code. In Dr. Geneser's words that meant he would go full court press to do whatever was needed to keep Linda alive. The plan was the same as in June; once Linda could not be involved in the decision, I would make the call as to what would be done. Dr. Geneser said he had seen this work for us before, and if that's what we wanted, then that's what he would do.

He asked us to make a decision by Monday that would dictate our path forward. The options as he explained them were to continue with full code and move to a skilled nursing unit (rest home). The second option was to go DNR (do not resuscitate), which would mean going to a nursing home or going home with hospice. It was quite sobering to realize the time we had known would come was here. I don't think we talked about it at all that night; we just sat there and enjoyed each other's company.

Saturday morning was fairly quiet, but that afternoon discussion turned to the matter at hand. Linda started telling me what she wanted (belongings) everyone to get. She just really wanted someone to want her stuff. She talked about what belonged to Grandma Sasser and Gma Hansen. We talked a little bit about the options but didn't really come to any conclusion. I expressed the fact I didn't want to do the nursing home, and she hesitated. I asked her why she would want to go to a nursing home. Her answer was usual for her; she was thinking of others. She was concerned where the family would respite at a nursing home. She was also concerned that if she passed away at home, people would feel funny about coming to the house and how I would feel. I told her we would all be OK with it.

We Knew This Day Would Come!

Sunday morning, November 5, 2006, she was about the same. No activity took place until we were forced to move her, and it was terrible. She could not breathe, and I could see the panic in her eyes. It scared me to death! Once we got her settled again, she was still struggling terribly to catch her breath. She looked at me with huge eyes and said, "I believe this is it." I asked, "Do you mean right now?" and she said, "Yes." I held her hand, and we prayed. She managed to finally catch up, but this was the closest she had ever felt to dying. We sat there a while, and she started talking.

She looked at me with the biggest innocent eyes I have ever seen. She said, "I don't think I can go on." I said, "Linda you don't have to." She said, "I'm sorry I can't stay longer, I'm sorry I can't fight anymore, but I'm so tired of working for every breath." Those words "work for every breath" just stuck in my mind. She apologized for leaving me by myself and so wanted to stay with me. I couldn't believe she was lying there apologizing to me. I told her that she didn't owe any of us anything and that she had fought way longer than any of us would have. Then, she looked at me and asked if it was OK for her to go. Really! I can't believe this; she is asking me for permission to leave. It was more than I could take. I burst into tears, and I was apologizing to her now. She said that's alright and maintained her composure while I lost mine. She said we knew this day was coming. It was 2:10 PM.

I said if we are making a change here, I could get her some help. She asked me how and I told her if we were saying this is it, I would order morphine. We were not using morphine because it slows down the breathing, and that's not something she needed. She said yes she would appreciate it. I called to order it and had to call the nurse four times before they got it to her. For some reason the nurse's phone battery was dead. It was 2:20 PM. This was the only real time we had any trouble, and it was at the worse time it could have happened. Morphine is a wonderful drug in that it tricks the brain so that it doesn't feel the lack of oxygen or the buildup of gases. Linda's biggest fear of dying was feeling like she was being smothered. Morphine would prevent that sensation.

We talked about changing the orders to DNR, and as soon as the first nurse came in Linda reminded me to get the papers signed. In fact, the nurse came in another time and Linda asked, "Where are the papers?" Once we made the decision, I was holding her hand, and for some reason I laid my other hand on her head. I prayed like I have never prayed before. The closest I have ever come before was at a Promise Keepers convention in Houston. The words flowed and flowed, and it was as if I didn't have control of the words. I guess I didn't, and the Holy Spirit was just flowing through me. I can't think of any other way to explain it, but just to say it was awesome.

I was bawling, and words were just flying out of my mouth. I'm not sure I can remember half of it, but I do remember Linda crying out to Jesus. She was praising God and invoking the name of Jesus. I know it lasted for about five minutes, and during that time the nurse's aide came in and left, and we never slowed down. I'm not sure what he thought, but he didn't stick around long. When I said amen it was as if a huge load had been lifted from my shoulders. I kissed her on the forehead and walked over to the window where I composed myself a bit.

After some time to gather myself together, I pulled out the Bible and just started thumbing through it for some scriptures. This was it! We made the final decisions that would mean we were in our last days together here on this earth. I needed God's word to comfort both of us and to reassure me that we had done the right thing and that we would see each other again. God's word didn't let us down. I read from Matthew and James 1:5–6, Proverbs 3:5–6, and Second Corinthians 12:8–10. Then, I found Psalms 103 and read

We Knew This Day Would Come!

the entire Psalm. It just seemed to fit, so, I read it again. It really spoke to me, and I still read it once or twice a week. Linda was really relaxed and quiet, but would smile when I made comments about what the scriptures were saying to me. Since I had requested the morphine, she was relaxed now. Once the decision was made, it became about comfort and care. The morphine was an option that we would and could use in that situation.

    I sat in the room thinking about what lay ahead. There would be many things to take care of, and one thought that came to mind was a funeral or memorial service of some kind. I knew what Linda's wishes were and that she had asked in lieu of flowers that donations be made to the veteran's association. As I considered all this, it came to my mind how much Linda had helped so many people, especially single moms. She would always have us fixing something for a single mom or painting their house or something. She just had a soft heart for single moms and children. There was never a woman walking down the road that we didn't have to go back and give a ride to. They would usually have a load of groceries or a couple of kids in tow. I can't tell you how many cars on the side of the road she would try and get me to stop and help.

    I thought how great it would be to use the money that people would spend on flowers that wouldn't last, and instead, spend it on something that would last. Then, the Linda Lawrence Helping Hand Fund idea was born. This was a very practical idea that was right down Linda's alley. I talked to Brother Mark about it, and he was in agreement to set up an account at Oak Ridge Baptist Church with the idea of helping single moms, widows, or wives of deployed soldiers. I talked to Linda about it and told her what I wanted to do. She said if that's what you want to do that would be fine.

    We set up the account and have helped several people with the fund, and it is still going today with donations made just about every time there is a funeral and people are made aware of the account.

And so the final week together on earth began. Kenda and John were headed down with the kids. They arrived about 10:00 PM Sunday night and came to the hospital. I tell you, those two kids just lit up Linda's face. She loved them so much. I hope I can someday get them to understand how much. Colby came in the next day and arrived about 10:00 AM on Monday. Kenda and Ethni joined Brother Mark, JW and me Monday morning.

Dr. Geneser showed up, and we started talking about our decision. He had seen the DNR before he came to the room. We told him we wanted to go home and have hospice come to the house. He was obviously upset and like everyone else his admiration for Linda would cause him to force back emotions that he didn't want to show. We told him we had discontinued all meds and were ready to have the feeding tube removed. He said we could leave the tube in for nutrition and we both asked him why. He just couldn't stop trying to save her, and I think his oath wouldn't allow him to think any other way. He said he would get things started. We could go home that night.

I can't even remember how long it had been since Linda had eaten; seemed like it was Thursday last week. The morphine had relaxed her, and she was feeling better since the kids were here. The ambulance was lined up, and hospice was coming to the house that night. Linda had told Colby she wanted a chicken fried steak. I just kind of laughed at the idea, but Colby said, "That's what she wants." I told him when we got her home and settled in bed, he could go to Roadhouse to get her one.

Hospice showed up, and there was a lot going on. Seemed like three nurses were there, and I was completing tons of paper work with two of them. When you have hospice, it is just like checking into a hospital. Colby went to pick up

We Knew This Day Would Come!

the chicken fried steak and Linda chowed down on it. So it would stay hot, he would take small portions into her room and help her eat. He just kept making trips, and as I sat at the dining room table, I was just amazed at each trip. She ate almost all the meat, potatoes, and the rolls. We were just all laughing.

We had an absolute angel for a hospice nurse. I have to go back in time to explain how God provided her. Julie is our neighbor. We had never really met her, and after we learned more about her, we learned why. She is a hospice nurse that pretty much lives with dying people. She was the best I have ever seen or heard of at what she does. Linda was reluctant to have hospice and to have someone else besides me taking care of her. Julie walked in and immediately straightened out the sheets on her bed. Linda's eyebrows raised, and she looked at me and said, "That's what a bed is supposed to look like." We have had some history about bed covers through the years, but that's another story. She said, "I like her."

Now, how we ended up with her. When Colby decided to go back to school, we told him we wanted to help. If he was coming back to Corpus, we would provide a place to stay. We immediately started looking for a house with an apartment in the back. We found a couple and actually bid on one but did not get it. We found the house on Timbergrove with the detached garage in the back. Both of us saw the answer to our needs. We could convert the garage into an apartment and the problem was solved. We bought the house and proceeded to convert the garage into an apartment.

We were still living out of boxes and had been for a few years since the move to the river. I sat down to watch TV one night and we started looking around. We both asked, "Why did we buy this house?" Neither of us liked it. We finally realized we didn't even look at the house because we were blinded by the possibilities of the detached garage.

How strange that both of us would not see the obvious things about this house we didn't like. I guess God blinded us.

Time passed, and one day I saw the kids that lived next door loading up as if they were moving. I went over and talked to the young man. He said yes they were buying a new house and that his aunt owned this house and wanted to sell it. I said I might have a buyer. I drove over to Daddy's and told him the house was going to be available. I asked him if he would be interested in moving there from his house on Wagonwheel. He replied, "Yes!" I started gathering information and was surprised at the size of the house. Looking at it no one realized it was as big as it is. When I told Daddy about the size, he lost interest. He said he didn't want to live in that big of a house. So the deal was off.

I thought about it for a couple of days, and then another idea came to me. I went to Daddy and said what about moving to the house we are currently in and Linda and I move to the big house. He said that would work. Julie lived straight across the street from the big house.

We Knew This Day Would Come!

Keith, Linda and Daddy –Jess Willard Lawrence

Let's go back to Monday night, November 6, 2006. Everything finally settled down, the nurses had left, and everyone was in bed. I was still sleeping on a pallet next to Linda's bed, and I'm so glad I had. Little did I know that night I would get the sweetest memory I have of that week and maybe for five years. Linda's morphine doses were minimal. She was very coherent and knew exactly what was going on. She was looking over the edge of the bed at me and said, "Hold my hand." I rolled over so I could reach her and held her hand. We held hands for a minute, then, she looked at me and said, "I love you so much." Those words would be the last really coherent words she would say to me. God is so good.

Tuesday, Linda decided she wanted to move to the couch in the den. We moved her, and she stayed in there the rest of the afternoon. When it came time to move her back to the bedroom, she wouldn't go. She said, "I want to be in here with all of y'all." She slept that night on the couch. Since the nurses were staying twenty-four hours a day, I had moved to a pallet in the front room.

I guess it was Wednesday night that I had my last real confirmed communication with Linda. One thing she had always said was she didn't want to feel like she was suffocating. I know some people don't like morphine for whatever reason, but it is a miracle drug when it comes to tricking the body. The doctors had assured Linda that the morphine would trick the body into believing it did not need oxygen and she would not get the sensation of suffocation. The hospice nurses, who were great, had slowly been increasing the amount of morphine so real communication was not going to happen. I thought sometimes she could hear me, but then it would turn out to be false.

Since we had made the decision Sunday not to fight this anymore, we all knew what this time was all about. It was a time to say good-bye, and we had all done that. So, I had to start distancing myself from her. I didn't really know what was going on in her head, but felt like if I kept trying to communicate with her, it might just make it harder on her to let go. We had reached the point of no return, outside of another miracle, and this is what she wanted, what we all wanted. I will never forget how she asked permission to quit fighting. That meant I had to quit as well, and we were there.

Still there was lots of activity in the house. Kenda, John, Ethan, and Ethni were there. Ethan was running up and down the halls like he likes to do. Someone was worried about the loud yells and shouting, but I said if she can hear it, she is enjoying it, so let him go. The hospice nurses stayed in the room and took excellent care of her to make sure she was comfortable.

I would go in the room sometimes and ask what they were doing and what they were looking for just so I could understand what was happening. The strange thing was the signs they were looking for never really showed up. Imagine that; Linda did it differently than most other people!

I had been sleeping on the floor in the front room since John and Kenda were in my bed. The nurse came in at 6:00 Friday morning, November 10, 2006. She said, "Hurry, she is going!" By the time I got there she was already gone. I stood there by the bed looking at her and thought "Now you can finally rest; what a battle!" I told her I loved her so much (her words) and kissed her on the forehead. I called Kenda out of the bedroom and told her, and we hugged. I then called Colby, who was staying at my sister's house down the street.

I could only thank God for this last week. What a way for things to finally end. We had family around all week, and everyone had their own chance and way to say good-bye. Most of all, we were all able to say good-bye. I don't see how it could have been any better.

We had all the arrangements lined up. In fact, when I went to the funeral home about six months earlier to give them her name, they already had a file. It seems Linda had gone to the funeral home about three and a half years ago and taken care of the arrangements. I knew nothing about it. She wanted to be cremated. She had me talk to some of the family members who she thought might have an issue with the idea. There were no issues with anyone, and I wondered what would have happened had there been. I mean, she did ask. That was just how she was always thinking of others. I remember in San Antonio when Dr. Angel said there was nothing else that they could do for her, the first words out of her mouth were, "Can I donate my organs?" Of course, she couldn't because they were all burned up with the years of chemicals she had taken to stay alive.

Mr. George and an assistant came to pick her up in about twenty minutes after we called. Mr. George knew Linda, and I could see that he was visibly upset. The doorway and hall to the bedroom where she laid were too narrow. So they couldn't get the gurney down the hall and had to carry her out. I know this had to be extra hard on him.

So, it was done, and what a relief it was to get that part over with. I don't mean to sound harsh, but the last thing Linda or any of us wanted was that it would drag out. Now, we could all move on, and that wasn't going to be easy. It was surreal that the journey had come to an end. I often thought I was dreaming and would wake up anytime and it would all be a bad dream.

Kenda and Colby jumped on the memorial service and had already most of it planned out. I had let them know what I wanted, and they already knew what Linda wanted. It came together quickly and easily. I'm thankful for that. We held the memorial Saturday, November 11, 2006 at 2:00 PM. It was short notice, but anyone that was coming was already there, and I couldn't imagine waiting until Monday. We all needed to move on.

The service was great, and there were lots of people there. There would have been lots more but Flint Hills Resources was in a major turn-around and all employees were involved. Either working nights or days, there were many who didn't get the word in time or just couldn't make it.

Chapter Twelve

Moving On

I would like to express a word of thanks to the nurses and technicians, and say a word about them.

I have mentioned the doctors and how instrumental they were in the successful outcome of this story. I haven't forgotten the nurses and technicians but felt they deserved their own section. I have said before I am glad there are those that want to be nurses and technicians. These are a very special group of individuals who have caring hearts and an attitude of service. I don't see anyone getting well without them. They have the toughest job in the hospital. They must treat everyone with dignity and respect, even when everyone is at their worst. They get to see people at their worst due to illness, through medications, at the scariest point of a persons' life, and at the end of their life. I have seen patients give up and say "I wish I could just die," and nurses have to be encouragers. I've seen patients told they can't get a transplant or loved ones face the death of their family member, and the nurses were there for support. They also have some good times to share when a patient gets better and goes home. As soon as one leaves healthy another sick one is waiting to come in.

Fair Weather Ahead

I have heard plenty of negative comments about nursing care slipping ,and it's not what it was, but I'm not willing to admit that. Nursing is just like any other profession where there are good and bad employees. There are those who have ended up as a nurse for one reason or another and probably should not have. But they don't have that market cornered, either. I have spoken to several nurses about how they handle the emotions of their job. In some cases, they get to know the patient and family very well. They see the good, the bad, and the ugly, and like it or not, they can become attached. Granted, some are easier to like than others, but that's on both sides. I have cried and laughed with several different nurses, and because we have spent so much time with them, we have a unique relationship.

If you spend enough time with any group of people, you learn the politics involved. Unfortunately, it seems people can't be together without politics. I think this is what gives the appearance and attitude of apathy, and it's understandable from anyone who has been in those situations. I think some nurses stay stern and what seems unconcerned because that's how they cope with these relationships. They can't handle the constant in and out of sick and dying people. I have to say I understand that one.

Over time you get your favorites and not-so-favorites. I know we waited many shifts to see which nurse or tech would walk in the door to be our assistant that day or night. Reductions of the work force have impacted the nursing community like other industries, and it seems they are always shorthanded.

I don't think I can convey adequate thanks that we have for the nursing staff and technicians who helped us in our deep time of need. It can be very demoralizing to be so helpless and have to depend on others for simple daily task. But when you meet those individuals who can help, making you as comfortable as possible, you know they have done something special. Not only the knowledge, but also the care is important when you are looking for help to stay alive.

My suggestion is to not settle for inadequate service due to lack of knowledge or even attitude. Positive reinforcement goes a long way and the nurse/techs usually don't get enough. I can't imagine how much negative feedback they get every day when they come to work. Just try to remember stress, fatigue, and emotions are pushing everyone to the point of breaking, and the patient has to come first. Hug your nurse or technician!

It is October 13, 2009. It is twenty-eight days until the three-year anniversary of Linda's death. I have had a desire to get this book completed but really couldn't work on it until six months ago when I sent Betty Black the first series of e-mails. Betty is my cousin Gene Black's wife. She is a retired professor from Texas A&M-Kingsville and had offered to edit the book for me. I always had it in the back of my mind, but somehow other things kept me from starting on the project.

Betty Black in the middle with her
husband Gene and cousin Mary

It's been quite a learning experience for me living by myself the past three years. As the story point outs, I had never lived by myself since I moved straight from my parents' house to our house. I struggled at first wondering what I was supposed to do with the rest of my life. There were many dark nights that I bounced around the empty house. I found much comfort and peace in scripture when I found the open Bible on my dresser every night.

I penned many poems and letters, some of which survived and others were thrown away. Again, the writing was therapeutic, and I enjoyed getting my thoughts out so I could see them. It helped me deal with the loneliness and uncertainty that I faced.

There was a regular routine each morning that started out with me falling out of bed to my knees asking God for some direction. Often I would end up on the bed or floor bawling about my situation. I would cry out to God, "What am I supposed to do now?" He finally gave me an answer after about ninety days.

One morning, I'm lying on the bed sideways and asking for guidance when God speaks to me in a very clear way to work with youth. I'm thinking and telling God you have the wrong number. He says no I want you to work with the youth. My next response is "Why would I do that; I don't even like them?" He said you will, and, in fact, you will love them. I was still a little skeptical, but it was clear He wasn't going to give up.

I went to talk to Pastor Mark and told him the story and said I would start working with the youth. He accepted the idea easier than I did. So I could get acquainted with them, I told him I would go to camp with the youth that summer. Since I didn't know any of them, and they didn't know me, it was a little strange.

Camp was great, and we really hit it off well. We came back from camp with a new perception of each other. God had given me a love for them and gave them a love for me. God was right, again!

I poured myself into that ministry and still do today. It has been one of the most rewarding ministries I've been involved in. The other opportunity God placed in front of me was the Shoreline Bible Study. Julie Guenter and I would go to this drug/behavioral rehab center every Monday and share from God's word. This has been life changing for me. I see so many girls that have had no chance, and most of the time it was by no choice of their own. God has blessed so many girls and us for this time we have given. Since I am the first male to my knowledge that was allowed to minister in the girls section of the unit, it was extra special.

Since experiencing these events, it's amazing how much my perspective on life has changed. Material possessions have no real meaning for me now, and I cherish the little things like time with friends, family, and God like never before. I still think of Linda often and have even dreamed about her in the last couple of months. She was and still is a big influence in my life, and I don't ever want to lose that influence.

I think one reason I have struggled with the completion of this book is I was afraid this part of my life would be over, and didn't want it to end. The truth is it is time to close this chapter and move on. I haven't had huge issues dealing with the experience, and I am thankful now for having lived through it all. It's made me a Godlier person. That is to say my relationship with God has bloomed to heights that I hadn't known before. I will always carry the accounts of what happened and be willing to share with anyone who wants or needs to hear them, but this part of my life is finished. I am richer because of it.

If this story has in any way encouraged, blessed, or helped to give God all the praise and glory, then it is a success. Nothing in this story is meant to reflect on me personally. The strength and perseverance to stay strong and withstand all came from God and Linda. She was so much stronger than me, and without God's undying love and support I wouldn't have made it.

Someone asked me once what I miss the most and after some thought, I realized what it was. What do I miss the most?

Intimacy! Guys will read this and the first thought is, yeah, I would miss the sex too. They could be no further from the truth. The intimacy I'm referring to surpasses the physical side of intimacy. I have considered what true intimacy is and have come up with this definition. Simplified, it is this: the highest level of communication possible between two beings. It's important to realize this level of communication is not limited to physical beings. I think this is why it surpasses the physical aspects of intimacy. It is in a spiritual realm that we experience the greatest true high level of intimacy.

True intimacy is not only knowing every infinite detail of someone, but loving them for those infinite details. Many times it is said I love you in spite of those details, but reality is I love you because of those infinite details. Not expecting the details to be examined with judgment, or held up in contrast to my own, but just loving them because the details are what they are. It makes it possible to be totally naked physically and spiritually without fear of ridicule and to be comfortable in true, complete, unrestricted openness.

I realize now, in hindsight, our intimacy grew more in the last four years of our life together than the previous years. Oh, there was growth during the first thirty two years, but it was slow and arduous. I think the reason it was so slow is that we spent more time building intimacy in the physical realm than the spiritual. I take the blame for that. Being a man, I desired more of the physical intimacy and ignored the spiritual aspect. Now, I realize how much I really missed by ignoring the importance of the spiritual intimacy. I'm convinced that had I been willing to connect in total spiritual intimacy, the physical intimacy would have been that much greater.

I can't even put into words what the last four years were like. Other than the holding of hands and touching through physical hygiene such as brushing her hair or bathing her, we had no physical contact, especially sexual. We connected on a level that far exceeded any physical connection we experienced in thirty-two years. God blessed us with the opportunity to experience true intimacy that we had not known before the last years together. I am so thankful to God for blessing us with those four years. A love grew out of that pain that cannot be explained. What scares me the most is thinking that had this not happened, we could have spent our time here on earth without knowing that kind of love.

So what is there to teach out of this experience? Two main lessons emerge that are obvious to me. The first lesson is a couple needs to understand the different levels of intimacy and pursue them with a defined goal in mind. We can't just muddle around in our relationships thinking it will all work out. Men need to realize there is another level and know that true happiness and contentment cannot be found for them or their mate without communicating on that level. There is something greater than the physical world.

The second lesson is God wants an intimate relationship with us. Now, I have had the time to cultivate an intimate relationship with God, and it is greater than it has ever been before. It is beyond anything you can imagine. Oh, how I miss the intimacy Linda and I had those last four years, but God has filled that void with a love that supplies all my needs beyond my dreams. He has given me a new sense of being and existence. He provides me the encouragement, means, and sustenance that give me purpose, direction, and passion to live the life He wants me to live. Now, I understand more of what heaven will be like. It's exciting to know that we will have total spiritual intimacy without the obstruction and hindrances of physical intimacy. Don't misunderstand that I am suggesting physical intimacy is not important and that I don't miss it. I encourage it among married couples, but I know that it can be better than imagined if it is second in the intimacy discoveries. That is why it is so important to refrain from premarital sex. We should know each other on a higher plain before we enter into the physical plain.

I continue to see where pain leads to true spiritual intimacy as well. When we, physically or spiritually, share hard times or pain, we grow closer. Look at army buddies who went through war battles together. Wounded and dying, these men and women have a bond that exceeds anything someone could dream up. They have connected at a time and place that only they can understand. In that understanding, they achieve a higher level of intimacy. Christ, Linda, and I share an experience that is only ours. Others share similar times of sickness and hardship, but each one is unique to their experience. Since all pain is subjective and there is no real way to measure, one is not worse than the other. But all of us share in a parallel experience that allows us to relate to each other. I will say that there is a certain level of pain and hardship that must be experienced to understand the high tide grieving that the loss of a spouse or child brings on. Now, I understand better than ever the sacrifice my Lord and Savior made, and the pain He felt. I'm not suggesting my pain was anywhere on the magnitude of His, but at least now I have a glimpse of that pain. I have connected with my Jesus on a new level that gives me a deeper understanding of those around me. Now, I can love more like Christ wanted me to love.

May 2005

Hands

One day, the hands on that old clock will reach the time we must say goodbye.
For we all know there is a time to love & live and a time for us to die.

But as I've watch those hands go round through so many years,
I think of all the time we had and rejoice with joyful tears.

Time is unforgiving not waiting on any man the way it marches on,
Either a bum in the gutter or a king upon his throne.
The hands of time were gracious for us, maybe not what we felt they should be.

But plenty to see the loving hands that nurtured our family tree.

Lost to men but understood above, a love that only Mom's would know.
The tender touch of a Mom's hands through which much love would flow.

The hands of a loving Mom who tended to scraps on knees,
The same safe hands that helped the kids up and down those "monster" trees.

The loving hands of a humble wife that brought peace to a scarred up old man.
Those hands that caressed the heart and soothed the pain as only God's blessing can.

So consider your time and know that a minute can seem like an hour,
Harder to grasp is how fast time flies and we realize it is not under our power.

We can't stop the hands from circling that old clock as it continues to sing out tick- tock, tick-tock.

But we can be mindful that time is as precious as our families and it will be gone way too fast,
So love and hold them like today is going to be your last.

While not all my time I spent wisely, I'm grateful for the time I spent with your loving hands.

I'm most thankful that while I held you in my arms, Jesus was holding us in His nail- scarred hands.

So ends this chapter of my life I like to call the Linda chapter. I have turned the page and moved on to the next chapter. Just like going into the previous chapter, I do not know what the title of the next chapter is or what will happen. I do know that I trust God, and each day I submit to his leading because only he knows what the story is about. After all everything that has happened or will happen is no surprise to him

I believe there might be some that will read this story and realize they have never enjoyed such peace or powerful prayers as recorded in this event. The peace and power described during this journey are a result of being in a relationship with God the Father. God loves each and every one of us more than we can comprehend and desires to know each of us intimately. Knowing the creator and entering into a relationship with Him that provides an eternal life with Him is not complicated or magical.

There is a long-time referenced group of verses commonly known as "The Roman Road." I have listed those verses below and encourage anyone who does not know the Lord Jesus Christ as their personal savior to read through these verses for a very clear explanation of how you can receive Him as Lord and savior. My prayer for everyone who does not know Him is that they will come to know Jesus and enjoy an eternal relationship that will provide peace and power for this life as well as the next.

Romans 3:23: For all have sinned and fall short of the glory of God.

Scripture is clear that "all" have sinned; that means every one of us are sinners. We cannot enter into a relationship with God if we have sin in our lives.

Romans 5:8: But God commendeth his own love toward us, in that, while we were yet sinners, Christ died for us.

God loved us before we turned from our sin. Just think about that: God loved you before you loved Him or even acknowledged his existence.

Romans 6:23: For the wages of sin is death, but the gift of God is eternal life in Christ Jesus our Lord.

It is clear in this verse that eternal life is a gift. If it is a gift, then it is something we cannot earn. Salvation is given through God's mercy, not something we can do to earn it.

Romans 10:13:... Whosoever shall call upon the name of the Lord shall be saved...

Romans 10: 9—10:... because if thou shalt confess with thy mouth Jesus as Lord, and shalt believe in thy heart that God raised him from the dead, thou shalt be saved: for with the heart man believeth unto righteousness; and with the mouth confession is made unto salvation.

So there it is a very simple plan that will lead you to a life-changing relationship with a loving God. If you have read these verses and desire to follow God and become a child of his, tell Him. Just call out to God, and tell Him you want to change the direction you are headed. If you have been headed away from God down the wrong road, turn around. Tell God you don't want that life any longer and head in His direction. If you decide to do these things, share it with someone. Find a good bible teaching church, and get involved in it. We need each other to make it through the tough times as described in this story.

Moving On

John 3:16: For God so loved the world, that he gave his only begotten Son, that whosoever believeth on him should not perish, but have eternal life.

> ### Perspective
>
> I am standing on the shore. A ship spreads her sails to the morning breeze and starts for the ocean. I stand watching her until she fades on the horizon, and someone at my side says, "She is gone!"
>
> "Gone where?" The loss of sight is in me, not in her. Just at the moment when someone says, "She is gone, there are others who are watching her coming." Other voices take up the glad shout, "Here she comes!"
> And that is dying.

Poem by anonymous author.

Linda would have this poem framed and she gave it to friends and loved ones when they had experienced the loss of someone special in their own lives. I had to include it.

Why? – God does calls some to make a sacrifice for the good of others. It the even greater honor of those he calls to Make the sacrifice –

The people are rare who cannot fulfill God's requirement for sacrifice that will be for the Good of his purpose –

Only in the greatest of tribulation will we selfcentered humans draw close to the Spirit of God – Our spirits must be shattered and Broken – we must become "poor in spirit" to know the Kingdom of Heaven –
– Then we can draw closer, intimately close to God's Spirit – In the greatest sacrifice of Your Servant – we get a glimpse of The Heart of God & Jesus and compassion of God for man – How much he would suffer for us –

"Blessed are those who mourn. They will be comforted"